JESUS' CHURCH

AND THE BOOK OF LIFE

ALBERT J. KAUSCH

Note for Librarians: A cataloguing record for this book is available from Library and Archives Canada at www.collectionscanada.ca/amicus/index-e.html

ISBN 1-4251-0324-3

Printed in Victoria, BC, Canada. Printed on paper with minimum 30% recycled fibre. Trafford's print shop runs on "green energy" from solar, wind and other environmentally-friendly power sources.

Offices in Canada, USA, Ireland and UK

Book sales for North America and international:
Trafford Publishing, 6E–2333 Government St.,
Victoria, BC V8T 4P4 CANADA
phone 250 383 6864 (toll-free 1 888 232 4444)
fax 250 383 6804; email to orders@trafford.com

Book sales in Europe:
Trafford Publishing (UK) Limited, 9 Park End Street, 2nd Floor
Oxford, UK OX1 1HH UNITED KINGDOM
phone +44 (0)1865 722 113 (local rate 0845 230 9601)
facsimile +44 (0)1865 722 868; info.uk@trafford.com

Order online at:
trafford.com/06-2081

10 9 8 7 6 5 4 3

JESUS' CHURCH

ACKNOWLEDGEMENTS

I WISH TO EXPRESS MY GRATITUDE and appreciation to Helen, my wife, for listening and proof reading my many drafts of this work. Pastors John Givens and his wife Alice and Tom Mithen, a former associate at the Knolls Atomic Power Laboratory, who became a man of the cloth, for entertaining my early essays of "The Seven Churches of Revelation", which could have been an alternate title.

Also in the course of my "walk" there have been many special friends who had influence upon my life, both living and dead, of whom I would like to acknowledge: Walter and Dee Sankowski, Marian and Bob Holt, David and Jane Stevenson, Jim and Shirley Grabb, Dan Hollenbach, Jim Dove, Mary Belle Dove, Lib Huckabee, John and Betty Dennis, Dave and Raeanne Snyder, Andy and Connie Terhune, Darlene and Terry Dildine, Pastor Bill Gavin, Pastor Julian Riddle, Ross and Linda Ripple, and Albert E. Kakretz.

We have been blessed with five loving and respectful high achieving children, Michael and Barbara, Albert Paul, Margaret and Mark, Joseph and Christine, and Susan and John. I want them to know that: "I have no greater joy than to hear that my children walk in truth." 3 John 3.

CONTENTS

JESUS' CHURCH

PREFACE

T HIS BOOK RECORDS THE AUTHOR'S convictions regarding the seven churches of Revelation and other related beliefs. It represents views held by the author on many subjects which are not widely discussed, probably because many of the topics are controversial or sensitive to some Christians. The book was initiated because I wanted to at least record my views on the various topics because the material incorporated has been on my heart for a long time and hence are important to me, and perhaps it will prove to be of some help to others. Hence, it represents a testament of my beliefs, which are based on a literal interpretation of the scriptures, to the best of my ability. I pray that the Holy Spirit concurs with my views on the Bible and will strengthen one's belief in the scriptures; and certainly there is no intention to weaken faith.

The ignominious worldly author of "The Prince" only made unpopular observations of real political situations. He was truthful but he was held in contempt none-the-less. Some of the concepts described in this book may seem threatening no matter how well meaning, hence: "There is nothing more difficult to handle, more doubtful of success, and more dangerous to carry through than initiating change. The innovator makes enemies of all those who prospered under the old order, and only lukewarm support is forthcoming from those who would prosper under the new. Their support is lukewarm partly from fear of their adversaries, who have the existing system on their side, and partly because men are generally incredulous, never really trusting new things unless they have tested them by experience. In consequence, whenever those who oppose the changes can do so, they attack vigorously, and the defense made by others is only lukewarm. So both the innovator and his friends come to grief."

~Niccolo Machiavelli, The Prince, ~ 1513.

I have no agenda to initiate "change" anywhere but I would like to point out that there are "differences" with theological teaching, but I don't believe there to be any scriptural deviations. If I thought the differences to be ultra-important, I would form my own church, but I'm realistic enough to recognize that no one would join up.

JESUS' CHURCH

INTRODUCTION

T HE APOSTLE JOHN WRITES THE Book of Revelation of Jesus Christ while in exile on the island of Patmos around AD 94-96. He sees a vision and he is told to write what he sees. The "Revelation" is written to seven existing churches located in Asia Minor or contemporary Turkey. The seven churches run the gamut of possibilities in the first, twentieth, or twenty-first centuries. They represent the various types of churches which exist throughout the church age. Christ has a message that is relevant for the ages concerning the churches.

After the books of Moses, Isaiah, Jeremiah, and other prominent authors of the Old Testament, we have been given Matthew, Mark, Luke, John, Paul, Peter, and others in the New Testament. They all contributed mightily to the story that God tells. However, in effect, Jesus, the Son of GOD writes the ending. That is, Jesus has the last word.

Churches have been organized and administered in accordance with scriptural requirements; nevertheless, it is clear that Jesus was not pleased with all of the results a mere 60 years after His ministry. In a sense, the Book of Revelation is really the Book of Jesus Christ, the Son of GOD. Jesus knew His people and he also knew the world; He wasn't surprised that most churches were far from being His church.

The resurrected Jesus speaks to His friend John with a

soothing voice, like rushing water. He is described as being dressed in a white robe reaching down to his feet with a golden sash around his waist. His head and hair are white as snow, and his eyes very penetrating ---- like blazing fire. His feet, and presumably his hands, the only parts visible to John, glowed like un-oxidized bronze. His face was even more brilliant, as John described it, like the sun in all it's brilliance. Nowhere else is there such a clear picture of Jesus, the Son of God who is alive evermore.

Jesus states to John that it is He, for the record, that holds the keys to death and Hades and no one else. Presumably then He holds the keys to "life" and heaven. Jesus is correcting the record as some have presumed that Peter holds the "keys". No; Jesus' Church is built upon the foundation of Jesus Christ and only He determines where we will spend eternity. Everyone has eternal life somewhere and Jesus decides where that will be; He has the keys.

Jesus spoke to John in the Revelation as God of things that needed to be prophesied to complete the Word of God as "out of His mouth came a sharp double edged sword". This means that that which is told to John are indeed God's Word: "the Word of God is sharper than any double-edged sword, it penetrates even to dividing soul and spirit ---, it judges the thoughts and attitudes of the heart. Nothing in all creation is hidden from God's sight ---." Hebrews 4:12. When Jesus spoke, He spoke the Word of God which is sharper than a two-edged sword.

John was afraid of the appearance of the resurrected Jesus he saw and heard. But Jesus assured him that He was Jesus, his friend, and he was not to be afraid and just write what you have seen in the past and what will take place sometime in the future. In the end of Jesus' revelation to His friend, Jesus says: "Come! Whoever is thirsty, let him come; and whoever wishes, let him take the free gift of the water of life." A promise for anyone and everyone, rich or poor, Catholic or Protestant, black or white, Muslim or Hindu, Presbyterian or Baptist, Jew or Gentile, it makes no difference. If you have received Jesus and His teachings by faith that he is who he said he is, then you are qualified to be a member of the true church, Jesus' Church, and a brother or sister to one another. Obviously, there is also an opposite view: those that do not accept this free gift will not live, spiritually. It is a free-will choice that each of us must make! Jesus is the first and the last, the alpha and omega; there is no more and there is no less according to the Book of Jesus.

The thief-on-the-cross who acknowledged Jesus as God received Jesus' free offer of eternal life with God in Paradise: that's grace, and John and all believers know that Jesus is their advocate with God, His Father, and our Father. The thief was indeed a thief; not a good man that spent his life in prayer and working at social causes. He merited condemnation as we all do; however, Jesus offered him eternal life for simply acknowledging Him as the Son of God with his mouth.

Having been born-of-the-Spirit, the thief was a new person who's character would have become that of every Christian. Yes, every Christian is indeed blessed with every promise Jesus gave in the Sermon on the Mount. Christians possess the character or attitude of those who worship the Father, His Son, and are in-dwelt with Their Spirit who brings them back to the will of the Father and Son when they sin! The thief wasn't around long enough for his character to be affected or to be corrupted by extra doctrine.

Most Christians, when they are called home, would like to have an audience with Jesus, Paul, Peter, David, Ruth, Esther, or Joseph of the Old Testament, or many others for a variety of reasons. Of course we want to see our loved ones and friends or people we admired in life: Bobby Richardson, a former Yankee, Billy Graham, my sister Lorraine, my children, my friends

Walter and Dee, friends Andy and Michele from the Front Street Deli from Georgetown, SC and Jim and Shirley Grabb, my lifelong friend. But the first person I want to see is the thief on the cross, who was crucified with Jesus. This will confirm my hope that Jesus loved a sinner like me as much as He did the thief. Whew, I'm in heaven after all.

The seven churches are often portrayed chronologically as corresponding to some time frame based upon some characteristic of that church. This concept is probably not correct seeing that all of the various attributes of the churches have always existed throughout the ages. A "church" represents a body of believers, not a building of a denomination.

The seven churches located in Asia Minor are listed below in the order they appear in scripture:

- Ephesus
- Smyrna
- Pergamos
- Thyatira
- Sardis
- Philadelphia
- Laodicea

According to reference (1) , the order of presentation was geographic; a traveler might reach them in the listed order. It is obvious that Christ chose the churches to represent a special problem that would prevail against Him down through the ages. Just as Paul's Epistles, though addressed to individual churches, are also intended for the entire church, so these seven messages also apply to the entire church in every age because they will always have similar troubles. Christ didn't search out large influential congregations, but churches with problems that He wanted to address. The problems and the messages to the churches are timeless. I have chosen to treat the "churches" in a different sequence to emphasize the point that Christ makes regarding acceptable and unacceptable worship.

Each letter is addressed to the angel or pastor of the churches with the admonition to read and take to heart the revelation of those things that are past, present, and future. The past referred to the birth, death, and resurrection of Jesus. The present refers to the age of the church from Pentecost to the rapture of Jesus' church. The future refers to the events after the Great Tribulation, until His second coming and beyond. Each letter ends with a threatening statement to pastors to pay attention to His words and be aware of those things that are not edifying; "He who has an ear let him hear what the Spirit says to the churches". The messages are clear. No church or pastor can be unaware concerning their responsibility regarding unacceptable practices, given that these letters were addressed to them.

The church age ends with the sounding of the trump of God, the physical resurrection and the rapture of His church, including the believing few or remnant, from contaminated, corrupt, dead, and lukewarm churches of the earth. The "world" is not much different from most of the churches of Revelation; except the church of Philadelphia, which He loves.

It is revealing and awesome that omniscient Jesus knew in AD 94-96 that believers in Him would abandon Him as the center of their worship, concentrating instead on politics, idols, social problems, and false teaching. Of the seven churches there were only two groups of believers in 94-96 AD and also 2006 AD which keep the scriptures and acknowledge Him. Within the other churches, there are rare believers which accept the scriptures and His name; they are generally called a "remnant of the church".

The Revelation of Jesus Christ represents a warning to

deviate professing Christians and encouragement to those that keep His word and acknowledge His name, or love the Lord for who He is and what He did for each of us. Possessing Christians are promised to be resurrected and protected at the trump of God. They are given a glimpse of heaven and the heavenly host and after the great tribulation and the battle of Armageddon they will return to earth to reign with the Lord for 1000 years. In the end, the Revelation of Jesus Christ is about His second coming and dealing with sin and Satan.

As we approach the end of the church age, the differences between Christian groups have become more acute, but there has always been a chasm between the church that concentrates exclusively upon the Trinity and those churches that have other interests and agendas. The churches of Philadelphia and Smyrna are different and set apart from the churches of Pergamos, Thyatira, Sardis, Ephesus, and Laodicea in the first and twenty-first centuries. There will be no Christian unity; indeed, the Bible indicates that there will always be substantial differences and no one can change the last word proclaimed in the Book of Jesus as He indeed has the last word, the alpha and the omega. Mohammed, and the Islam he subsequently produced, are not from the Father and Son of the Bible.

The newspapers of our day take every opportunity to report on differences and schisms within various Christian communities. The secular media do not differentiate between groups, or denominations of "Christians". These differences are unmistakable, especially between the religious "left" and "right". The "left" has melded with the far left wing of the secular culture regarding feminism, abortion, socialism, animal rights, human rights, environmentalism, homosexuality, etc.. Radical feminism is the strongest force, according to Robert Bork[2] , as it strives to work within churches to re-image the gospels and replace them with a history and language pleasing to feminist' political correctness. To the religious left, political liberation seems to be more important than spiritual salvation. To the left, the conservative right are considered to be fanatics with values that undermine freedom and liberty. Actually, their principal offences are that they respect the scriptures and acknowledge Jesus as Lord and hence oppose abortion, normalizing homosexuality, and marginalizing the father within the family. According to Bork, Catholic bishops, with the exception of the abortion issue, often look like the liberal Democratic Party in robes, and mainline Protestant churches within the World Council of Churches, the National Council of Churches, and many others, are even further to the left. Bork is a practicing Catholic.

A mystery for the ages concerns the neglect or outright spurning by Christendom of the end of the story of redemption written in effect, by their Savior for them. The Book of Jesus is simply not studied or taught, even though God promises a special blessing for doing so. It is safe to say that all denominations endorse the Apostles Creed. Yet the "Creed" does not include the end of the story as He promises to: "come again and receive you unto Himself that where He is there you may be also". The most important part of any story is the end; Jesus promises to come again to finish the story as He is the Omega.

His prayer will finally be understood by everyone who speak the prayer, often without thought or understanding: "Our Father who art in heaven, hallowed be thy name, thy kingdom come, thy will be done on earth as it is in heaven, give ----". The conditions on earth get worse and worse culminating in Armageddon and His second coming, and then and only then does His kingdom come and will His will be done upon the earth.

According to Reference (1), "this portion of scripture has been completely neglected. While many turn to the epistles of Paul and other portions of the New Testament for church truth, often the letters to these seven churches, though coming from Christ himself and being climatic in character, are completely ignored. This neglect has contributed to churches not conforming to God's perfect will". On the other hand, Jesus understood the "world" and His adversary who stands against His church within some of His churches.

JESUS' CHURCH I

The Church at Philadelphia and the Attitude of Jesus' Church

THE FAITHFUL CHURCH

"And to the Angel in the church in Philadelphia write:

> *These things says He who is holy, He who is true, "He who has the key of David, He who opens and no one shuts, and shuts and no one opens": "I know your works. See, I have set before you an open door, and no one can shut it; for you have a little strength, have kept My word, and have not denied My name. Indeed I will make those of the synagogue of Satan, who say they are Jews and are not, but lie—indeed I will make them come and worship before your feet, and to know that* **I have loved you.** *Because you have kept My command to persevere, I also will keep you from the hour of trial which shall come upon the whole world, to test those who dwell on the earth. Behold, I am coming quickly! Hold fast what you have, that no one may take your crown. He who overcomes, I will make him a pillar in the temple of my God, and he shall go out no more. I will write on him the name of My God and the name of the city of My God, the New Jerusalem, which comes down out of heaven from My God. And I will write on him My new name. He who has an ear, let him hear what the Spirit says to the churches."* [3]

JESUS LOVES THE CHURCH REPRESENTED by the group worshipping in Philadelphia and warns enemies of His church that they will be subservient to them. Jesus and no one else holds the key to the kingdom, even though there are others who claim to hold the key.

The Church at Philadelphia is the example for all of Christendom to emulate. It is portrayed by Jesus: "I have placed before you an open door that no one can shut. I know you have little strength , yet you have kept my word (the scriptures) and have not denied My name". The door of this church is always open for Christ to enter the hearts of worshippers who worship in spirit and truth. Christ enters the open door provided for Him by the faithful. The door cannot be shut as Jesus will always be in their hearts: "This is the will of the Father who sent Me, that of all He has given Me I should lose nothing, but should raise it up on the last day"[4] . Jesus and believers in His church are wed forever; the bond cannot be broken.

By contrast, the door of the Laodicean church is closed and Christ is on the outside trying to enter. Evangelicals often quote the verse:

> *"Behold, I stand at the door and knock.*
> *If anyone hears My voice and opens the door,*
> *I will come in and dine with him, and he with Me."*[5]

In addition to Jesus waiting patiently for an invitation, He is outside one of His churches, which on the surface is absurd.

His church has "little strength". That is, by comparison with the forces at work in the other churches, and the world, this Philadelphian church has numbers that are relatively few or they are of "little strength". There are great numbers of professing Christians and many denominations, but there is only one true church, the Church of Philadelphia and their numbers are few, relative to the other churches and the world. But we should be mindful of Jesus great promise to His church that upon the foundation of only Jesus Christ, will His church be built [6]. The foundation of the church of Philadelphia is His Word and name. Christ speaks of a husband's love for his wife, which should be analogous to His love for His church[7]. He gave Himself for His church; the church of Philadelphia.

Born-again people are drawn to the Church of Philadelphia by the Holy Spirit and they are blessed by God to become new creatures; suitable for lives with God. Through the Holy Spirit, one believes that Jesus did accept my sin unto himself and He will intercede with the Father in my behalf, presenting me blameless and white as snow to the Father. I need no other defense. He did this even though I deserve nothing but condemnation. This was God's plan for the redemption of the human race.

Jesus knows His flock and their born-again outlook:

Blessed are those who depend upon God, for they are humble and mourn over their sin, even after we first believe, and submit to God through the righteousness of His Son, who washes them to be whiter than snow, again and again. They are forgiving because they have been forgiven; time and again. They love their brothers and sisters in Christ, and hence their neighbors. They hunger to know God and His Son through the scriptures. For their reverence toward God and His Son, they are reviled; but theirs is the kingdom of heaven and they will see God.

The attitude of a believer, paraphrased, and his relationship with God are defining qualities of the character of Jesus' disciples [8].

The characteristics of a Christian may be found in Christ' teachings in His very first sermon which is referred to as the

Beattitudes or blessed sayings. The Sermon on the Mount, was delivered to believers. To be a "believer", one must be born-of-the-Spirit. Jesus says in the book of John that a "person must be born again".

Every Christian has the "attitude" defined by the Sermon on the Mount; without exception.

To the "world" and some "Christian" churches, the Sermon on the Mount, taken out of context, is their "social gospel" where people identify with the virtue and compassion toward the "poor", the "mourners", the "meek", the "righteous", the "merciful", the "pure", the "peacemakers", and those that are "persecuted". The words by themselves seem right, but God meant something else.

POOR-IN SPIRIT

Jesus: Blessed are the poor in spirit, for theirs is the kingdom of heaven.

Interpretation: Blessed are those who recognize their spiritual poverty or bankrupt condition in spiritual matters; they then depend upon God for all things. Recognition of our poverty does much to manage our pride where we can be used by God. We must be able to see our sinfulness. God loves bad people, or sinners with open arms. All they need to do is "knock" on His door and He will meet and dine with them.

World: Blessed are the poor that have a broken spirit; the more broken, the more blessed. Obviously those who are not sufficiently poor, are to be despised. These poor are victims of the "rich".

God is not partial to the poor, the rich, or the "good" amongst us. God loves people that know they are sinners as a starting point. According to Romans: All, everyone, have sinned and come short of the glory of God.

THOSE THAT MOURN

Jesus: Blessed are those that mourn, for they shall be comforted.

Interpretation: Blessed are those that are sorry for their sin, or they mourn over their sin—they are profoundly sorry, as David mourned during his reconciliation with God in Psalm 51.

World: Blessed are those that mourn over their misfortune and the misfortune of others showing their sensitivity and care for other people.

THE MEEK

Jesus: Blessed are the meek, for they shall inherit the earth.

Interpretation: Blessed are those who are humble considering their "saved" condition since they have been saved by grace—no one can boast because they recognize their sinful condition; noting that all that ever lived were sinful, but everyone think themselves "good". There is no deed or work that we can do to "inherit the earth". We are saved by the grace of God, which is not merited. We are obligated to accept, or reject, God's only Son, a free gift to all of man-kind. He did it all; all we had to do was to accept or reject His free offer of everlasting life with Him and our brethren.

World: Blessed are those with gentle, compliant, mild-mannered, pious qualities. We often observe the very religious exude this attitude.

THE RIGHTEOUS

Jesus: Blessed are those who hunger and thirst for righteousness, for they will be filled.

Interpretation: Blessed are those who hunger and thirst for the entire story of God's revelation to men recorded in the Old and New Testaments. Only Jesus is "righteous". We have no appetite for the things of God before our spiritual birth and our "hunger and thirst" afterward is indeed satisfied as we are fed by the Word ---- we will be "filled" but we never stop "hungering and thirsting" to understand His Word.

World: Blessed are those that hunger and thirst for justice and equality. Egalitarianism is the doctrine of liberalism with outcomes that result in full political, social, and economic equality for all people. Even race horses are handicapped to come out equal and the ACLU in the name of justice works to undermine the ten commandments, marriage for only men and women, and the right-to-life for the not yet born. Worldly justice and equality of outcomes are more important in some so-called Christian churches than salvation. That is, when it comes to justice and equality, the world, even the "Christian" world have an insatiable appetite. They certainly do not "hunger and thirst" spiritually .

THE MERCIFUL

Jesus: Blessed are the merciful, for they shall obtain mercy.

Interpretation: Blessed are those that forgive injury of mind and body since they have been forgiven again and again for the sins that we have committed against God. Turn the other cheek, walk the extra mile. Judge not, but support law, order and the ten commandments.

Strive to ensure that punishment fits the crime. The punishment for murder is death. Forgive when appropriate but remember that we are not God and we do not have the power to forgive sin.

World: Blessed are those that are compassionate and sympathetic for any situation without due regard for the law and punishment. "Thou shall not kill", under any circumstances, is not scriptural nor "merciful" to victims and families.

THE PURE OF HEART

Jesus: Blessed are the pure in heart, for they shall see God.

Interpretation: Blessed are those that are sorry for their sin and are washed to be whiter than snow in the blood of Jesus. David's cleansing is symbolic and is recorded in Psalm 51. God never desired sacrifices; He only wanted an acknowledgement that He was God and the Creator. A pure heart achieved via a broken heart that acknowledged a need for Him is all God desired.

World: Blessed are the good-hearted people of the world who in the balance of things do more "good" than "bad". "Good" people will see God as good exceeds bad.

THE PEACEMAKERS

Jesus: Blessed are the peacemakers, for they shall be called the sons of God.

Interpretation: Blessed are the evangelists that brings God's message to the world. War makers hate; peacemakers love and those with the greatest love for mankind are those who bring God's saving message to a troubled world are called evangelists. Every person born of the spirit is an evangelist, in their own right. Billy Graham, and my wife, in my opinion, are great peacemakers.

World: Blessed are world leaders and statesmen who strive for peace with great acclaim.

THE PERSECUTED

Jesus: Blessed are those who are persecuted for righteousness' sake, for theirs is the kingdom of heaven.

Interpretation: Blessed are all believers since they will be reviled and persecuted because they acknowledge Jesus as the Son of God;. "they hated me before they hated you". Martyrs are examples of the most persecuted. See the Church at Smyrna in the Book of Jesus (Revelation). We are declared righteous through faith in Jesus. Jesus is always the problem with the hate of Christians.

World: Blessed are those that are criticized and persecuted because they seek justice and equality for the downtrodden victims and masses of the world. America and the "rich" and Israel and the Jews are often the problem.

SALT

Jesus: You are the salt of the earth.

Interpretation: Christians are the salt of the earth: a very special people that are nevertheless reviled for their beliefs.

LIGHT

Jesus: You are the light of the world.

Interpretation: Christians are the light in a very dark world.

We cannot boast concerning our relationship with Jesus as we earned nothing but condemnation.

The qualifications for church leadership are clearly spelled out in the Bible[9,10]. An elder must be blameless, husband of one wife, not overbearing, not quick-tempered, not given to drunkenness, not violent, not pursuing dishonest gain. Rather, he must be hospitable, one who loves what is good, who is self-controlled, upright, holy and disciplined. These qualifications need to be satisfied, but they are not enough because one could be "good", as defined by "Timothy" and "Titus" and still not be adequate "Christians", especially for church leadership. A "good" cult leader, Muslim, or lodge member could meet the Biblical qualifications of "Timothy" and "Titus". Five of the churches, with leadership that no doubt met Biblical qualifications, do not measure up to the church at Philadelphia. Why?

Born-again people are regenerated persons qualified to be associated with the Church of Philadelphia where they will be pillars in the temple of God. Their attitude, and their leaders, are exemplified by Jesus' very first sermon, the sermon on the mount. Born-again people understand His words and they are truly blessed as He promised. A Church of Philadelphia results when everyone in the congregation, even the leadership, are born-again with the attitude of the Beatitudes. When Paul wrote the qualifications for leadership, he apparently assumed that they were born-again, or Christian. Jesus, having the final word, condemned the wayward churches even though they probably met leadership qualifications; their attitude came up short.

Theologically, there are no frills or bells and whistles associated with the Church of Philadelphia, only the scriptures and Jesus. No other doctrine; it is that straightforward, and if any doctrine is more complex than the simple message it is probably not correct:

> *My hope is built on nothing less*
> *Than Jesus' blood and righteousness;*
> *I dare not trust the sweetest frame,*
> *But wholly lean on Jesus name .*
> *On Christ the solid rock I stand;*
> *All other ground is sinking sand,*
> *All other ground is sinking sand.*

The Church of Philadelphia will not endure the Great Tribulation. Jesus promises to keep them; "from that hour of trial which will come upon the earth". Some "Christians" will not endure the plagues and suffering of that seven and one-half year period, where over half the population of the earth will perish, according to the Revelation. They have a secure place in heaven , being sealed by the Holy Spirit, and are the pillars of His kingdom.

Jesus will have a new name in glory and His remnant people from the Church at Pergamos will also have a new name given to them by none other than the Lord Jesus; but the new name is known only to him who receives it. It is assumed that all believers will be given a new name. The old refrain may have spoken to this heavenly reception: "There is a new name written down in glory and it's mine"; however, it is written on the soul and not in some ledger to celebrate the salvation of some person.

Jesus' new name will be a surprise. We know that he will have a new title: King of Kings and Lord of Lords, which is written on His thigh, but His new name is "known only to Himself". Revelation 19:12.

The Pearl of great price parable refers to salvation which is hidden from most people but it is so valuable that people who have it revealed to them are willing to give up all that they have to possess it; a picture of the Church of Philadelphia [11].

Be sure that your place of worship is a Philadelphia type congregation of born-again people where the name of Jesus is above all names and His word is studied and followed. Just as it was when Jesus revealed His Book of Revelation, perhaps one church in six or seven will be a congregation of His people or a Pearl of Great Price which is rare but within reach. With experience as my teacher we have found Philadelphian churches in various denominations; i.e. some Brethren, Community, Baptist, and Presbyterian churches. The key is not the denomination, but whether the believers are born-again and hence worship in spirit (enthusiastic reverence) and truth (God revealed in the scriptures).

JESUS' CHURCH II

THE CHURCH AT SMYRNA: RESULTING FROM HATRED OF GOD AND HIS PEOPLE

THE SUFFERING CHURCH

"And to the Angel of the church in Smyrna write:

> *These thing says the first and the last, who were dead, and came to life: " I know your works, tribulation, and poverty (but you are rich); and I know the blasphemy of those who say they are Jews and are not, but are a synagogue of Satan. Do not fear any of those things which you are about to suffer. Indeed, the devil is about to throw some of you into prison, that you may be tested and you will have tribulation ten days.* **Be faithful unto death, and I will give you the crown of life.** *He who has an ear, let him hear what the Spirit says to the churches. He who overcomes will not be hurt by the second death"[12].*

GOD IS OMNISCIENT SO JESUS gives assurance to the beleaguered church at Smyrna that He knows their plight and the suffering that they are experiencing for upholding the name of Jesus. There is no condemnation of this church. In fact they are promised a crown of eternal life, or no spiritual death, as their reward for faithfulness to His name and Word. This church is called the suffering church.

The world reviles and hates God, and hates Christians because of Jesus: "If the world hate you, you know that it hated Me before it hated you"[13], "and all who desire to live godly in Christ Jesus will suffer persecution"[14]. And: "He who hates Me hates My Father also"[15].

Christians should not be deceived by the world and their politicians and propagandists. They are not on the Lord's side and "He who is not for Me is against Me"[16].

From the very beginning, there was enmity, or hatred, between Satan and his world and God:

> *"And I will put enmity*
> *Between you (Satan) and the woman (Eve),*
> *And between your seed (unbelievers) and her Seed (Jesus Christ);*
> *He (Jesus Christ) shall bruise your head (Satan's),*
> *And you (Satan) shall bruise His (Jesus Christ) heel."* [17].

Christians continue to be persecuted, harassed, and reviled for their belief in Jesus and His word: in China, in Islam where there are over 1000 million Christian persecutors, the United States liberal left wing, and throughout the world. The world and even deviate "Christianity" hate those fundamentalist' who keep His Word and acknowledge His name.

The first death is physical and the second death referred to is spiritual; the suffering church is eternally saved hence there is no second death.

U.S. President George W. Bush has experienced the re-birth, spoken of by Jesus. This qualifies him for heaven in the after-life, but hatred on this earth. For this reason he is reviled throughout the world. Mr. Bush is a Christian but he knows that the world is not, and he also knows that nations cannot be converted, only individuals. He turns the other cheek to individuals, but imposes Old Testament standards on the world. Praise Moses, David, the Lord, and Mr. Bush.

Faithful believers must expect persecution and suffering from a world that rejects God; it's part of the territory. "Those who are not for Me are against Me". The church at Smyrna is composed of born-again believers in Jesus Christ, like Philadelphia, and for that reason it is persecuted.

JESUS' CHURCH III

The Church at Sardis and The Book of Life

THE DEAD CHURCH

"And to the Angel of the church at Sardis write:

> *These things says He who has the seven spirits of God and the seven stars: I know your works, that you have a name that you are alive, but you are* **dead**. *Be watchful and strengthen the things which remain, that are ready to die, for I have not found your works perfect before God. Remember therefore how you have received and heard; hold fast and repent. Therefore, if you will not watch, I will come upon you as a thief, and you will not know what hour I will come upon you. You have a few names, even in Sardis who have not defiled their garments, and they shall walk with* **Me** *in white, for they are worthy. He who overcomes shall be clothed in white garments, and I will* **not** *blot out his name from the* **Book of Life**; *but I will confess his name before My Father and His angels. He who has an ear let him hear what the Spirit says to the churches."[18]*

SEVEN IS THE PERFECT NUMBER corresponding to the Lord Jesus, who makes this proclamation to the church at Sardis. There is no commendation for the church at Sardis; it is described as being "**dead**" which is the condition in the body when the heart stops. This church is composed of people that are not regenerated or born-again, which is the heart of Christ' church. There is no hope unless they change and listen to the Lord and He will come as a thief does, or quickly; there being a difference between quickly and soon. It is obvious that Jesus did not come soon as it has been greater than 2000 years since His first coming. Watch and be ready for his return. This church never had a heart for God.

There are various reasons people join in church fellowship, in addition to love of the Lord. That is, there are many social, political, and economic reasons for people to attend club meetings and concerts.

It is probable that Sardis is composed of unbelievers who are unable to understand the scriptures[19]. The Holy Spirit is not operating; hence there is no prayer, no Psalms or hymns, no praise, no love, and no evangelism; they are basically dead. The dead church has not received the Holy Spirit and cannot:

> *"Praise God from whom all blessings flow,*
> *Praise Him all creatures here below,*
> *Praise him above ye heavenly host,*
> *Praise Father, Son, and Holy Ghost".*

Yet there are a few in Sardis who are believers and are deemed to be worthy. There are a few in the body of Sardis that live and can be useful in the true body of Christ; the Church of Philadelphia, the church whom Jesus' loves because they acknowledge His name and Word.

III A. THE BOOK OF LIFE -- ONLY GOD IS
TO BE WORSHIPPED

Life is short and eternity is forever and each day we live we are one day closer to eternity. According to the New Testament we have a choice of either spending eternity with God and His saints in heaven, or paradise, because of the blood of Christ, or we can chose to spend eternity in hell with the Devil and his associates by rejecting His sacrifice. You pick the names of the most ignominious and imagine eternity with the likes of Nero, Hitler, Stalin, or Ted Bundy.

Legalistically we refer to Old Testament or New Testament dispensations; which are the ordering of events by divine authority. In fact though, there a number of other possibilities which must be considered. There have been many millions of peoples that do not neatly fit either category --- what happens to every soul is important to God. Under which dispensation, Old or New Testament, are various peoples at various times saved: for example, take the period before the O.T., the period between Jesus birth and His resurrection, fetuses, babies, or children before the "age of reason", and folks who were never given an opportunity to receive Jesus in the far flung regions of the earth before the present age of mass communication? There may even be others, but just thinking about aborted fetuses and the plans that God may have had for him or her breaks the hearts of Christians everywhere. Where are they and who loves them? God loves them and His love is eternal and infinite.

In Old Testament times people were saved by worshipping God. In New Testament times people are saved by worshipping God; they are lead to God by the Holy Spirit and they are saved by worshipping the Father via the Lord Jesus Christ. When you see the Son you are vicariously seeing the Father; such is their relationship. There is now and there has only been one criterion to be saved; worship God, the God of Israel!

It has been said that Old Testament Jews, upon death went to the bosom of Abraham. It has also been said that Godly Old Testament people, before the coming of Christ, were saved by the blood of Christ or His saving grace was retro-active. Confusing and probably not true, and we know that there really are no people that deserve anything but condemnation. But surely, Moses, Joseph, David, Elijah, Jeremiah, Job, Noah, and the blessed mother of the Lord Jesus Christ are in heaven spending eternity with God and His only begotten Son.

We have evidence that Old Testament believers reside in heaven given the encounter of Moses and Elijah with Jesus on the Mount of Transfiguration as witnessed by James, John, and Peter, as recorded in Luke 9 and Matthew 17. God also spoke to the three witnesses that Jesus was His beloved Son and they should pay attention to Him. Jesus was resurrected, with a multitude of witnesses, but Moses and Elijah also live, and they together form the basis for our hope. It is important that we realize that Moses, Elijah, and Jesus knew each other well; they were spending eternity together before Jesus came to earth to shed His blood for sinful people and to be resurrected as He had promised. He also promised us that if we believed in Him we would never perish either, and we too would have everlasting life.

God is obviously sovereign and can do anything He wants, but there is no doubt that I desire that God have a system that ingeniously include everyone at every time without special conditions or circumstances for God is consistent, fair, and just for all peoples.

This seems to be consistent with scriptures for God is quoted similarly: "The Lord is not slack concerning His promise, as some count slackness, but is longsuffering toward us, not willing that any should perish but that **all** should come to repentance. **2 Peter 3:9.**"

The only way to do this is to include everyone from the outset, or conception!

There is no evidence in the Bible that people are ever written into the Book of Life after having received the Lord Jesus Christ; there is, however, rejoicing in heaven: "In the same way, I tell you there is rejoicing in the presence of the angels of God over one sinner who repents. **Luke 15:10.**" Yet as heaven is described in the Book of Jesus, there will be no person there that have not been written in the Book of Life; **Revelation 21:27.** This could mean that names were written in at some time during a persons life, or God wrote them all in at conception and did not blot them out during their lifetime for not worshipping God and His Son. Everyone is included, if the latter were the plan.

Islam has 73 sects of the Shii religion and it represents only 10% of Islam's one thousand two-hundred million souls. "Christianity" probably have similar variations of Christ' church because of the importance that some give to various passages of scripture and false teaching. Strip away man- made doctrine and we are left with Jesus' Church, the Church of Philadelphia. Worship only God.

No study Bibles or theology, of which I am aware, teach that everyone is written into the Book of Life at conception although it is logical and all encompassing and somewhat scriptural, whereas the alternative has no basis. It is only important conceptually, but very important because every living person then has the same opportunity to worship God and for Jesus to take our sin. Christianity is not a club of the saved as anyone has the same opportunity given the role of the Holy Spirit to convict sinners ---- all sinners. Jesus came to save sinners, all sinners, at any time during their life.

In the book of Exodus, after the Israelites and Aaron practice idolatry by worshipping the golden calf, Moses pleads for leniency with God:

> *"Oh what a great sin these people have committed!*
> *They have made themselves gods of gold.*
> *But now, please forgive their sin --*
> *But if not,*
> *Then blot me out of the Book (of Life) You have written."*

God replied to Moses:

> *"Whoever has sinned against Me,*
> *I will blot out of My book."*[20].

Do not worship false gods or idols. This message is clear in the Old Testament as the chosen people, time and again, indulge in the practice. The longest book of the Bible, Jeremiah, devotes perhaps 95% of its contents to warnings against the most important , or atrocious, of all sin. The Jews finally got the message; but only after the dispersion of Israel; however, they still have not embraced God's Son, which is equivalent.

Of great significance is Jesus' promise to believers at Sardis not to blot their names from the Book of Life. The Book of Life refers to the "roster of the righteous who are to inherit eternal life"[21]; these are the saved that can never lose their salvation[22]. No one can be blotted from the Book of Life if they worship God; the Lord Jesus Christ. However, unbelievers, obviously, were never part of Christ' church and by implication could be erased from The Book.

Man was created spiritually to always offer devotion to something or somebody. Hence, man either worships false gods, idols, or God. Examples of false gods are Allah as in Islam,

Buddha, ancestors, or even humanity itself. Idols take the form of images or symbols of the creation. That is, unbelievers are not worshipping God, hence they worship something or somebody else.

In order to blot out or erase a name, it first must be recorded in the book. Hence, all souls conceived are initially in the Book of Life. Unbelief is cause for God to erase their names at death, leaving only believers in the Book. This has been true since Adam and Eve and includes all the saints of Old and New Testament times. God has always had the same criteria for souls to be saved: idols and false gods shall not be worshipped; only God.

From the very beginning God knew us, even before we were born or had any form, He entered everyone's name in the Book (of Life):

> "My frame was not hidden from You,
> When I was made in secret,
> And skillfully wrought in the lowest parts of the earth.
> Your eyes saw my substance,
> Yet being unformed.
> And in your **Book** (of Life)
> They all were written (everyone's name),
> The days fashioned for me (the length of my life),
> When as yet there were none of them (before my birth)"[23].

Clearly, every name is recorded in God's Book of Life at conception and all of the days that we will be given. And then what? Revelation 3:1-6 indicates that believers will be kept in the book and unbelievers may be blotted out from the book. There is no one in heaven not in the Book, Revelation 21: 27 . Anyone not found in the Book of Life are cast into the "lake of fire", Revelation 20: 14-15.

God will not accept idolatry or blasphemy of His Holy Spirit and considers those practices to be foolish and indeed evil. He will not tolerate them and certainly will not live with those who do not repent of this worst of all sin. God considers idolatry, and or false god worship, and blasphemy to be equivalent:

> "---- your fathers have **blasphemed** Me by being unfaithful to Me (through worship of idols).
> When I brought them into the land concerning which I raised My hand in an oath to give them,
> And they saw all the high hills and all the thick trees,
> There they offered their sacrifices and provoked Me with their offerings.
> There they also sent up their sweet aroma and poured out their drink offerings"[24].

Jesus was asked by a certain lawyer:

> "Teacher what shall I do to inherit eternal life?"
> He said to him, "What is written in the law?
> What is your reading of it?"
> So he answered and said,
> "You shall love your God with all your heart,
> With all your soul,
> With all your strength, and with all your mind,
> And your neighbor as yourself."
> And He said to him,
> "You have answered rightly; do this and you will live"[25].

Jesus asks a contemporary individual, obviously before His passion, what is necessary to gain eternal life. The individual's answer is essentially "Worship God". This individual is speaking from the point of view of the Old Testament ---- and Jesus obviously represents the New Testament and the Old Testament. This exchange between the lawyer and Jesus points out an essential truth of God ---- His criteria for eternal life has always been the same throughout all the ages---- worship only God [47]. Once Jesus came as the Son of God and the Holy Spirit was commissioned after Pentecost; to "Worship God " now meant to worship the Father, Son and Holy Spirit.

There can be no doubt that the great commandment[26], referred to by Jesus, had it's roots in the first of the ten commandments given to Moses [27]:

> "I am the Lord your God (Father, Son, or Holy Spirit).
> You shall have no other gods before Me.
> You shall not make for yourself a graven image or
> Any likeness of anything that is in heaven above,
> Or that is in the earth beneath,
> Or that is in the water under the earth;
> You shall not **bow down to them or serve them**".

God keeps track of the name of every soul from Adam and Eve, through the times of the prophets, and Jesus' life on earth before and after His ministry and resurrection, to the present age. There are no special conditions before, during, or after Jesus.

God, through the prophet David, gives some insight into His simple formula for people to be suitable for a life with Him and His Son:

> "Who may ascend into the hill of the Lord?
> Or who may stand in His holy place?
> He who has clean hands and a pure heart,
> Who has not lifted up his soul to an **idol** (or vanity/ nothingness),
> Nor sworn deceitfully"[28].

Paraphrasing: For GOD so loved His chosen people that He promised life with Him, if they acknowledged their sin and requested forgiveness with a broken and contrite heart, if they only worshipped Him and did not blaspheme His Spirit.

He gave us, again through David, the means by which man can be purged of his sin to become "whiter than snow" with a "clean heart". God did not desire sacrifice; He desired: "a broken spirit and a contrite heart" Given a proper heart attitude, God was pleased with sacrifices on His altar for the forgiveness of sin [29].

The Old Testament spells out as clearly as possible God's problem with, and the consequences, of idolatry and or the worship of false gods:

> *"See I have set before you today life and good,*
> *Death and evil,*
> *In that I command you today to love the LORD your God,*
> *To walk in His ways,*
> *And to keep His commandments,*
> *His statutes,*
> *And His judgments,*
> *That you may live and multiply;*
> *And the LORD your God will bless you in the land that you*
> *go to possess.*
> *But if your heart turns away so that you do not hear,*
> *And are drawn away,*
> *And worship other Gods and serve them,*
> *I announce to you today that you shall surely* **perish**" [30].

The consequences for disobedience regarding commandments six through ten are national stagnation; however, worshipping and serving false gods results in the most severe punishment possible.

That is, the Israelites will perish; like they never existed, they will be blotted from the Book of Life. A Christian cannot lose his salvation, he was sealed in the Book of Life by the Holy Spirit; hence he will never be even tempted to worship anyone but the Father and His Son. When you see the Father you see the Son. Axiomatically, worship God (Father, Son, and

Holy Spirit) and live forever as Jesus promised; worship false gods and die spiritually and invoke God's wrath as promised in Romans.

The New Testament speaks to the word "perish" similarly: "For God so loved the world, that he gave His only begotten Son, that whosoever believeth in Him should not **perish**, but have everlasting life".

The opposite of a people who "perish" because of worshipping and serving false Gods is that they will be "saved" by worshipping and serving only God. In the Old Testament people were saved as Job was saved. Job loved God!

God speaking in the Old Testament saves those who worship Him and not those who worship idols or false gods: "I have left Me seven thousand in Israel, all the knees which have **not bowed** unto Baal and every mouth which have not kissed him". [57]

Obviously, there is no greater sin than to sin against God by worshipping someone or something else, and there is no greater punishment than to be blotted from His Book. Returning to the account between Moses and God concerning retribution for the "golden calf " episode, God heard Moses' plea and did not blot them from His Book; He brought a plague against them as punishment but they were not blotted from His Book, the ultimate punishment. They were chastened for the "golden calf" episode. However, the account does not reveal the action God takes at the end of their lives. Did they change and worship Him exclusively or did they revert again to some form of idol worship which would have been cause for individuals to be blotted from the Book, at that juncture.

III B. WORSHIP JESUS, THE SON OF GOD

Jesus is the Son of God; hence He too is God and the name of Jesus can be used in the Old Testament commandments: "I am your God (Father, Jesus, and Holy Spirit)" or "You shall love the LORD your God (Father, Jesus, and Holy Spirit) with all your heart, with all your soul, and with all your strength". According to Macarthur [31], the use of LORD signifies a clear statement that there is only one God, or monotheism. Word experts indicate that the word for LORD implies unity (the trinity) and not singleness. Hence, the Godhead would be an appropriate interpretation for the use of the name "God" in the commandments. Hence, Jesus also is God of the Old or the New Testaments; hence, Jesus too must be worshipped to satisfy God's criterion to worship God in lieu of false gods or idols.

Jesus was with the Father from the beginning; he was there when the Prophets entered in His kingdom. He knew Moses and Elijah when He met with them as they discussed the plan for the redemption of man at the "transfiguration" [32]. " No man (ever) came to the Father but by Me"[33]as "I Am the Way the Truth, and the Life".[33] That is, the Psalm of David, Psalm twenty-four, and John three-sixteen are in concert with each other:

> "For God so loved the world that He gave His only begotten Son,
> That **whoever** believes in Him should not perish but have everlasting life".[34]

Paraphrasing: For GOD so loved the Jews and the Gentiles that He permitted, and even planned, that His only Son would be a sacrifice for all peoples who accept Him as their God, and their names will not be blotted from the Book of Life and hence they will gain eternal life.

The name written into the Book of Life at conception is sealed by the Holy Spirit. Personal sins are put upon Jesus and the name can never be blotted out. The Bible says that God's motive is love for us and He grants us grace and we are sealed forever:

> *"In Him you also trusted,*
> *After you heard the word of truth,*
> *The gospel of your salvation;*
> *In whom also having believed,*
> *You were* **sealed** *with the Holy Spirit of promise,*
> *Who is the guarantee of our inheritance until the redemption*
> *of the purchased Possession, to the praise of His glory."* [35]

The LORD must be worshipped exclusively to gain eternal life. When the Father sent His Son to earth, their plan for redemption of the human race was set in motion and Jesus' sacrifice made it possible. Prior to Jesus coming it was necessary to worship God with animal sacrifice for the forgiveness of sin. The new covenant in the blood of Jesus is a better way and there are many benefits, comparatively, for "His yoke is easy and His burden is light":

- His sacrifice was sufficient and final to cover the sin of all people for all time.
- God's wrath for our sin was satisfied through the blood of His only Son.
- God's saving grace was extended to Gentiles in addition to His Chosen people.
- Jesus ascension made it possible for the Holy Spirit to come as a comforter and conscience for believers and to lead unbelievers to a time of decision.
- Whereas Old Testament worshippers at times backslid to idol worship; to worship false god's is no longer possible

for born-again redeemed people [36]as idol worship is cause to be blotted from the Book of Life. People who worship Jesus commit other sins; but they are protected from "false gods" and the worship of idols. Worship false gods and perish or worship Jesus and live: John 3:16.

- Being "born-again", or regenerated, seals a name in the Book of Life.
- Jesus' sacrifice rent the curtain of the Holy-of-Holies so that all of mankind now had access to God himself —through prayer.

Accepting Jesus and life seems to be a no-brainer, given the enormity of the reward, and ease, to just acknowledging Him as God and Savior. But, as humans we love sin and it comes in many forms and for each of us there are particular sins that are hard to give up; which we must, when we are joined to Jesus, and experience the spiritual birth. Many of the reasons people do not readily break with their sin are pride, lust, power, money, alcohol, possessions, false gods and idol worship, hatred of God, procrastination, family religious traditions, public humiliation and hatred by other people, and so forth. Saying before witnesses "I do" to the question: "Do you John Doe accept Jesus Christ as your God and Savior" is enormously difficult for humans and final; and if they stray they will be reminded by the Holy Spirit.

Accepting the Lord Jesus Christ is clear to the person that made the commitment; but no one else. Believers sometimes make gossip concerning whether this one or that one is indeed "saved" from their vantage point and observations. Like marriage, it is either "yes" or "no"; there is no "maybe". The Holy Spirit knows and he will do the convicting. Satan works hard at destroying a believer's witness, often using "prayer" and gossip to accomplish his goal.

Every person that is conceived is written in the spiritual Book of Life and will stay in the Book and see the kingdom of heaven if they worship God and accept the Son of God as their God; if they do not, they will be blotted from the Book of Life. In the Old Testament God promises to blot people out of The Book for worshipping idols or not worshipping Him exclusively. Similarly a few folks of the church at Sardis that walk with the Son will be dressed in white in heaven and were not blotted from the Book of Life. However, the majority of so-called believers at Sardis were dead to the Holy Spirit, the name of Jesus, and scriptures; hence risked being blotted from the Book of Life.

God writes the name of everyone in the Book of Life upon conception; God is fair, everyone has a chance [34,58]. The aborigines of Australia and New Guinea, the Eskimos, the American Indian, the aborted fetus, children struck down by disease or people on the highway of life, and the person in the next seat at the ballpark or bus, are all in the Book of Life. Every neighbor is important to God and He desires that all people become born again people and brothers (brethren). A neighbor today is a brother tomorrow. On the road of life during our journey we are all equal before God; not until the end are we separated:

> "And He shall set the sheep on His right hand,
> But the goats on the left.
> Then shall the King say unto them on His right hand,
> Come,
> Ye blessed of My Father,
> Inherit the kingdom prepared for you from the foundation of
> the world" [37].

The sheep are the brethren in Christ Jesus that were all goats or neighbors before being born-again. Hence treat thy neighbor as thyself, or as your brother, as indeed he may be. Also, grieving parents upon the tragic death of an infant often find fault with a "loving God". The good news is that those youngsters are in the Book of Life.

There is no evidence in the Bible that God writes a believers name in the Book of Life upon his acceptance of the Lord Jesus as his Savior. However, a man or women is "saved" regardless of when the name is written. But the concept is enormously important to defend fairness, justice, hope, and God. God must be perceived as giving everyone, over every time and place an opportunity to be "saved". That is, no-one was left behind because of God, and the sacrifice of His Son was for all peoples until they draw their last breath. Man is without excuse if all are written in the Book of Life upon conception. That is, no one is damned by God without cause.

Everyone has a choice; the aborigine can worship God as Job did and not the moon or stars. The twenty-first century person can accept and worship the Father and Son, and not blaspheme the Holy Ghost; thereby keeping his or her name in the Book of Life.

Psalm 24, in its entirety as expressed in "Today's English Version", illustrates Old and New Testament truths that show the power of God, His timeless criterion for salvation, and Jesus as Savior and King where He is at the gate to enter hearts victorious:

THE GREAT KING

The world and all that is in it belong to the Lord:
The earth and all who live on it is His.
He built it on the deep waters beneath the earth
And laid its foundations in the ocean depths.

Who has the right to go up the Lord's hill?

Who is allowed to enter His holy temple?
He who is pure in act and in thought,
Who does not worship idols,
Or make false promises.

The Lord will bless him;
God his Savior will declare him innocent.
Such are the people that come to God,
Who come into the presence of the God of Jacob.

Fling wide the gates,
Open the ancient doors,
And the great king will come in!
Who is the great king?
He is the Lord, strong and mighty,
The Lord, victorious in battle!

Fling wide the gates,
Open the ancient doors,
And the great king will come in!
Who is the great king?
The Lord of armies, he is the great king!

The similarity between the last two stanzas and Revelation 3:8 are striking and the apparent difference with Revelation 3:20 where the door is closed is worth noting:

"Behold, I stand at the door and knock. If anyone hears My voice and opens the door, I will come in to him and dine with him, and he with Me".

JESUS' CHURCH IV

CHURCH AT PERGAMOS; CHARLATAN LEADERSHIP OF A "JESUS" CHURCH

THE CONTAMINATED CHURCH

"And to the Angel of the Church at Pergamos write:

These things says He who has the sharp two edged sword: I know your works, and where you dwell, where Satan's throne is. And you hold fast to My name, and did not deny My faith even in the days which Antipas was My faithful myrtyr, who was killed among you where Satan dwells. But I have a few things against you, because you have there those who hold to the doctrine of Balaam, who taught Balak to put a stumbling block before the children of Israel, to eat things sacrificed to idols, and to commit sexual immorality. Thus you also have those that hold to the doctrine of the Nicolaitans, which thing I hate. Repent, or else I will come to you quickly and will fight against them with the sword of My mouth.
He who has an ear, let him hear what the Spirit says to the churches. To him who overcomes I will give some of the hidden manna to eat. And I will give him a white stone, and on the stone a new name written which no one knows except him who receives it."[38].

THE SHARP TWO-EDGED SWORD OF scripture refers to one side being able to save and the other to condemn. Jesus has the sword of salvation as well as the sword of death; and it is very sharp and it is decisively used for either purpose.

Pergamos is commended for not denying the name of Jesus, even when persecuted. This emphasizes the importance of Jesus name. It seems that just the act of acknowledging His name, reverently, is an important step to accepting Jesus as the Son of God and your savior:

> *"Nor is there salvation in any other, For there is no other name under heaven given among men by which we must be saved"[39].*

His name is far above every name ever given, even in the future, according to:

> *"God has highly exalted Him and given Him the name which is above every name,*
> *That at the name of Jesus every knee should bow,*
> *Of those in heaven,*
> *And of those on earth,*
> *And those under the earth,*
> *And every tongue should confess that Jesus Christ is Lord,*
> *To the glory of God the Father."[40].*

"Should" is a very large word, however, and pride and hatred prevent individuals from acknowledging His name, so that the numbers that do are few and mostly attend "Philadelphia" type churches. Pergamos is commended for having the faith to establish their church in the den of their adversary, Satan. Pergamos was known to be a center for the worship of idols and kings.

This message or instruction is all about the Old Testament pseudo-prophet Balaam (a Medianite) that operated in conjunction with Balak (a Moabite King) to avoid a war with a stronger Israel, as Israel was poised to enter the promised land. Balaam was very famous as a prophet and poet of the time. His merger with Balak consisted of a political mission to obtain a curse from God against His chosen people, Israel, for reward and great honor. God refused, so Balaam concocted a proposal for the seduction of Israelite men with Moabite women to defeat Israel; which would lead to spiritual contamination, and hence was forbidden.

The church at Pergamos had fraudulent leadership and used their office in perverse ways in the world. The church was contaminated with a counterfeit leadership as Balaam was a phony prophet. There is no Book of Balaam in the Old Testament. Politics are all about power, and religion is about spirituality and they are like oil and water. We see people every day on both sides of the political spectrum that parade in religious attire, and like Balaam, try to intercede to bring about some kind of compromise in difficult political situations. Sometimes they even claim to intercede with God on behalf of their flock. Fill in the names.

Do not permit the church to become contaminated with leaders who do not represent Jesus, but the world. Separation of church and state, or a church and political parties are essential. In contemporary terms, a church agenda that includes support of socialistic political principles on the one hand and conservative political principles on the other, are not a good idea. Churches must not allow themselves to be contaminated by worldly pursuits and social agendas such as women's rights, and even human rights. The church at Pergamos is the contaminated church; contaminated with worldly leadership for reward or political power. We have collections being made in churches to support political candidates, and political candidates electioneering from the pulpit.

The Church at Pergamos, and the Church at Thyatira, are singled out as having too much doctrine and simply acknowledging His name and following Him and the Father were not sufficient. Any additional doctrine is not acceptable as Jesus' possesses and expresses hatred in His revelation: "Thus you also have those who hold to the doctrine of the Nicolaitans, which thing I hate." God's hatred is reserved for sinful thoughts and ways, but God does not use or express "hatred" often. In another instance, on another contemptible topic, God speaks of the miracle of conception and birth in Psalm 139 and He immediately afterward gives His view, hatefully, of those who participate in the most blood-thirsty of all practices. I suggest that God foreknew the world-wide situation with regard to abortion in our time, especially:

> *"Oh, that you would slay the wicked, O God!*
> *Depart from me, therefore you bloodthirsty men.*
> *For they speak against you wickedly;*
> *Your enemies take my name in vain.*
> *Do I not hate them, O Lord, who hate You?*
> *And do I not loathe those who rise up against You?*
> *I hate them with perfect hatred;*
> *I count them my enemies." Psalm 139:19-22.*

It is indeed awesome and understandable that God would hate the most bloodthirsty act ever perpetrated by humanity. That He hates additional doctrine is also understandable given that anything extra to the worship of the Father and His Son is forbidden by the first and second commandments. Jesus is the beginning and the end; the alpha and omega, no more and no less. Hate is a strong word.

The doctrine of the Nicolaitans has been portrayed variously by Biblical expositors:

"The beginning of a distinction between the clergy and the laity and or a licentious sect led by Nicolas of Antioch, who advocated freedom in conduct and encouraged participation in pagan practices which culminated in the "doctrine of the Nicolaitans" in which promiscuity was incorporated into the activities of the church." Israel My Glory: July-August 2006, Charles E. McCracken, director of FOI Gospel Ministry, Brampton, Ontario.

Or:

"The doctrine of the Nicolaitans was compared to the doctrine of Balaam. Hearsay from antiquity holds that eating things offered to idols, encouraging idolatrous worship, and denying God as the creator of the world; giving that powers to others. Also something called a "community of women" was part of the doctrine which was highly licentious. Ungers admits that in the end "the real origin of the sect will never be ascertained with certainty." Ungers Bible Dictionary.

Or:

"An heretical Group in the early church who taught immorality and idolatry. Introduced pagan feasts and orgies into the early church. Mentioned in the churches at Ephesus and Pergamum. Ephesus resisted the doctrine." Holman Illustrated Bible Dictionary .

Or:

"The setting up of a distinct class of men called clergymen

and the denial of the common priesthood of all believers. Certain men lusting for religious power declared themselves above the rest of the people, upon whom they laid burdens, and virtually made them slaves of this self appointed group of religious dictators." Studies in Revelation by M.R. DeHaan.

Or:

"Similar to the teaching of Balaam. Identifies Nicolaitans as the followers of Nicolas, one of the first deacons discussed in Acts 6. The cult was involved in immorality and assaulted the church with sensual temptation. Their teaching perverted grace and replaced liberty with license." Macarthur Study Bible.

These commentaries and studies show a variety of speculation, portrayed sometimes as factual among experts regarding the sect or cult referred to by Jesus as the "Nicolaitans". They all seem to miss the point of Jesus' condemnation; nothing, whether of good or bad intentions is to be added to the alpha or omega that already was given by Jesus. No more and no less. In the end, the facts considering the actual doctrine are of little consequence; no additional doctrine is acceptable and no one really knows what the "doctrine of the Nicolaitans" referred to, and it doesn't matter.

As I read Biblical instruction by Paul and others, I am always alert for anything added to "help" Jesus. I find amplification and instruction of Jesus' basic teaching but no really new revelation that cannot be found in less detail in Matthew, Mark, Luke or John.

Jesus reminds this church that He has the sharp two edged sword that can either save or condemn; there are no other choices. Hence the leaders, and their followers, must repent of their contamination or Jesus will "fight against them", or judge them; in which case He cannot be their Savior and advocate, and they will be judged just as the world is judged, which is appropriate for the world, but not the saved of God. Facing God for my sins is a frightening thought without Jesus as my advocate. It should be noted that the Church at Philadelphia is not judged which is consistent with Christian theology of the saved.

Leadership at the Church at Pergamos is obviously not born-again or regenerated, and it is splintered and not authentic, and the result is a contaminated church; between "Balaam and Nicholas", the proverbial rock and hard-place. Jesus knew it and he told us that there would be charlatans operating in churches soiling His name. But there are those who overcome these very great obstacles and they will be rewarded by Jesus.

JESUS' CHURCH V

THE CHURCH AT THYATIRA; JESUS-PLUS: IDOLATRY IN HIS CHURCH

THE CORRUPT CHURCH

"And to the church in Thyatira write:

> *These things says the Son of God, who has eyes like a flame of fire, and His feet like fine brass: I know your works, love, service, faith, and your patience; and as for your works, the last are more than the first. Nevertheless, I have a few things against you, because you allow that woman Jezebel, who calls herself a prophetess, to teach and seduce My servants to commit sexual immorality and eat things sacrificed to idols. And I gave her time to repent, of her sexual immorality, and she did not repent. Indeed I will cast her into a sickbed, and those that commit adultery with her into great tribulation, unless they repent of their deeds. I will kill her children with death, and all the churches shall know that I am He who searches the minds and hearts. And I will give to each one of you according to your works.*
>
> *Now to you I say, and to the rest in Thyatira, as many as do not have this doctrine, who have not known the depths of Satan, as they say, I will put on you no other burden. But hold fast what you have till I come. And he who overcomes, and keeps My works (will) until the end, to him I will give*

power over the nations --

He shall rule them with a rod of iron;
They shall be dashed to pieces like the potters vessels --

As I also received from My Father; and I will give him the
morning star. He who has an ear, let him hear what the Spirit
says to the churches"[41].

THE CHURCH IS COMMENDED BY Jesus especially for their works that have become more intense with the passing of time. We don't know the nature of the works attributed to Thyatira, but it is speculated that they kept their sacraments with increasing frequency, fed the poor, and cared for the sick. Works and piety may have counted toward their attainment of heaven; hence, they had a passion for love, service, and faith in their church.

For by grace you have been saved through faith, and not of yourselves; it is the gift of God, not of works, lest anyone should boast. Ephesians 2:8-9.

The congregation at Thyatira mistakenly input the confused idea of earning salvation through good works as opposed to the free gift given by God to men which the Bible calls "grace". Salvation from beginning to end is "grace". There can be no mixture of grace and works, or else it would not be grace ---- which has been described as unmerited favor with God.

Rewards for faithfulness and practical holiness, such as habitual performance of the sacraments, are dispensed as rewards, but this is not to be confused with unmerited favor or grace.

Grace was conferred by God to the thief on the cross to accept the Lord Jesus Christ and that very day he was with the Lord in Paradise. God did His part and the thief did his: he acknowledged Jesus as God which he proclaimed with his mouth; he merited nothing and certainly received no sacraments nor did any good works to earn salvation. It was free, a gift of God.

We are taught in Bible study to look for recurring words in an account. In Jesus' message to Thyatira the word "works" is used three times. Jesus succumbs to the proposition of "works" and agrees to judge them by their works given that that was their desire. Ok, lets do it your way. Good works are but folly and not a stable foundation. In the secular world, what one man considers to be good another may think it to be evil or even irrelevant. For example, be a good steward and save God's earth from the contamination of greenhouse gases when in fact God may just have had the foresight to build enough margin in the design to accommodate change. The oceans are a great reservoir for heat and gas accumulation and they are probably sufficient to absorb any perturbation to His system caused by the crown of His creation. It is better to place one's faith on the solid rock of Jesus Christ rather than the sinking sand of works invented by men.

But there was evil in Thyatira, perhaps the clone of a person that ranks with the most detestable people of history; the wife of Ahab (Jezebel), a King of Israel of antiquity who:

> "did evil in the sight of the Lord, more than all who were before him"[42].

And as a result of massive idolatry:

> "There was no one like Ahab who sold himself to do wickedness in the sight of the Lord, because Jezebel his wife stirred him up. And he behaved very abominably in following idols according to all that the Amorites had done (homosexuality, bestiality, idol worship, and sacrifice of children), whom the Lord had cast out before the children of Israel."[43].

Jezebel's character was summed up at the end of her life by Jehu, her executioner and the King of Israel after Ahab, Ahaziah, and Joram;

Joram asked: "Is it peace, Jehu?" Jehu answered, "What peace, As long as the idolatries of your mother Jezebel and her witchcraft are so many" [44].

She was pushed by servants from a balcony into the path of Jehu's chariot and horses where she was trampled to death, and eaten by dogs so that all that remained were her skull, feet and hands, just as Elijah had prophesied.

No one names their children Judas, Adolph, or for that matter, Jezebel. Hence, the Jezebel of Thyatira is probably a pseudonym for teachers of idolatry and immorality in a Christian church. Therefore, the Church at Thyatira represents an abominable marriage of pagan beliefs and practices, which takes the form of false gods, idols, and doctrine emphasizing more than Jesus and additions to scripture. Jesus opposed new doctrine not in scripture, in His letter to Pergamos and here again to the church at Thyatira.

An idol can be any object given excessive reverence or ardent devotion. It may take the form of a Christian article of faith. Obviously, worshipping idols and at the same time, Jesus, is bizarre and inconsistent with God's first and second commandments; nevertheless, that's the way it was. Some articles of faith are endorsed by church leadership. Revelation is clear, worship: "Only God"!

Jesus' considered Himself a servant and He normally referred to His followers as His disciples or His children. Here, He calls out "servants" that have been seduced by the evil "Jezebel". That is, the leaders of the Church at Thyatira have been taught by "Jezebel" immorality and to also eat that which has been offered up to an idol.

No one but God is to be worshipped; ever. No "Christian"

can dispute the holiness or the authenticity of Peter, Paul and Barnabas, or angels attending the Apostle John, with regard to the worship of false gods; especially "Christian" false gods:

PETER IS NOT GOD

The Roman centurion, Cornelius, upon meeting Peter in Caesarea: "As Peter was coming in, Cornelius met him and fell down at his feet and worshiped him. But Peter lifted him up, saying, stand up, I myself am also a man"[45].

PAUL AND BARNABAS ARE NOT GOD

Paul, through the power of the Lord Jesus Christ healed a crippled man in Lystra. The people gave honor to Paul and Barnabas, referring to them as the gods Hermes and Zeus, greatly distressing them (Paul and Barnabas): "Men, why are you doing these things? We also are men with the same nature as you, and preach to you that you should turn from these useless things to the living God, who made the heaven, the earth, the sea,---. And with these sayings they could scarcely restrain the multitudes from sacrificing to them."[46].

THE ANGELS, EVEN IN HEAVEN, ARE NOT GOD

John, upon witnessing the greatness and the grandeur of heaven was overwhelmed: "And I fell at his feet (an angel) to worship him, But he said to me, see that you do not do that! I am a fellow servant, and of your brethren who have the testimony of Jesus. Worship God!"[47].

Can there possibly be anyone or anything more worthy than the people cited and angels to be excessively venerated or worshipped? Of course not: Worship God!

Over indulgence of "other sin", as described in Romans 14, is not akin to the worship of idols or false gods. To equate "other sin" with "worship" is insensitive of the gravity of the immense importance God places upon the first commandment. Indeed the central theme of the Bible is: worship God and live, worship (bow down and serve) false gods and perish, Old or New Testament. Other sin is not an idol nor is it a false god. Worship is a conscience decision by the worshipper to either live or perish which is a simple concept that seems to elude theologians that want to elevate other sin to the status of the first commandment which diminishes the significance of the first commandment. Commandments are not relative, but absolute.

Scriptures may allude to some situation where "sin" referred to by Paul becomes huge and turns into idol or false god worship. Offhand, are there any cases mentioned whereby "sin" becomes an idol such as, alcohol, drugs, or a prized camel? I don't think so although "money" is problematic as man cannot serve two masters; money or God. To serve, is an element of worship; but one must also hold up the "sin" to reverence and respect and bow down to it.

All sin is forgivable except blasphemy of the Holy Spirit which attributes to others the miracles of God. The most important miracle of all is the creation.

According to Unger's, blasphemy is also a state of hardness in which one consciously and willfully resists God's saving power and grace, which are also miracles of God.

Worship of idols and false gods were forgivable, but dangerous sin and is cause for damnation without repentance and restoration. Acceptance of Jesus as Lord and Savior (worship) prevents worship of false gods and idols. Hence, idol and false god worship are an Old Testament problem and a problem for the unsaved in New Testament times. Christians sin, but after having been to the cross of Calvary they are no longer tempted to worship Allah, the Man Up-stairs, the Great Spirit, Mary, Paul, the Bible, the friend, the bishop and his ring, or the Pope. Respect possibly, but worship no. Shadrach, Meshach, Abednego, and Daniel would not bow down to idols or kings, for to do so would have lost their soul, for what does a man gain if he gains the whole world and suffers the loss of his soul. Everyone has a choice to either worship God or something else. As John's Revelation angel said: "Only God". To know God is to fear Him; to know God is to love Him; to know God is to worship Him; to know Him is to obey Him.

Jesus promises the people at Thyatira that if they persist in being corrupted they will not be raised at the trump of God and hence, they will endure the three and one-half years of God's wrath that is inflicted upon the earth to redeem His people. This period is called the "great tribulation". Their sin is uplifting other gods to the very status of Jesus Christ, while venerating Him to a certain extent, and eating food they offered up to their idols, which denigrate the name of Jesus. Jesus refers to the church having made their bed in hell, so to speak, for not repenting of their immorality and problems with idols.

This church has worked hard to achieve salvation; hence, Jesus promises to fairly judge them according to their works. Fear of standing before God at the Judgment giving an account of my life makes me tremble thinking about it. Speech would fail. Even Job felt inadequate to argue with God, so who am I to possibly think that I could convince God of my inherent "goodness" and merit. The saved of the Church of Philadelphia are not judged, according to their works, because they believed on the name of the Lord Jesus. Jesus will intercede and act as an advocate on behalf of Christians. Thyatira never understood the basics: men are saved by grace not of works lest any man should boast. These folks were not saved and obviously their leadership were not saved either.

Worship of false gods and or idols is cause for spiritual death. Once more, be reminded that we will not perish if we exclusively worship Jesus—but we will perish if we do not. The popular John 3:16 says that if we worship God we will not perish but have eternal life, and by inference if we do not worship God, but idols or false Gods, we will be eternally damned. Also once we accept Jesus we are married forever; hence idol worship is not a problem for regenerated or born-again believers. For:

> "My sheep hear my voice, and I know them, and they follow
> me:And I give unto them eternal life; and they shall never
> perish, neither shall any man pluck them out of my hand.
> My Father, which gave them me, is greater than all; and no
> man is able to pluck them out of my Father's hand.
> I and my Father are one. John 10: 27-30."

Fortunately, we have a promise for the Judgment; that is, there is no judgment of believers:

> "Now to Him who is able to keep you from stumbling,
> And to present you faultless
> Before the presence of His glory with exceeding joy,
> To God our Savior,
> Who alone is wise,
> Be glory and majesty,
> Dominion and power,
> Both now and forever, Amen." [48].

Thyatirians designed a new "Christianity" with new doctrine added to scripture, that included Jesus and a whole lot more. Again, the church at Philadelphia represents the acceptable church:

> "You have kept My word and have not denied My name."[49].

More than Jesus is not acceptable for Jesus is the alpha and the omega; there is no more in the universe. In fact Jesus warns:

> *"For I testify to everyone who hears the words of this prophecy of this book: if anyone adds to these things, God will add to him the plagues that are written in this book; and if anyone takes away from the words of the book of this prophecy, God shall take away his part from the Book of Life, from the Holy City, and from the things that are written in this book."*[50].

Do not alter the conclusion of the gospel story nor add any elements of worship that diminish the worship of the Father, Son, and Holy Spirit. Even in Thyatira there will be some who overcome the very great obstacles imposed upon them by immoral leadership and they will be dressed in white with the Church at Philadelphia. Jesus is the "Morning Star".

V. A. DAVID: DEFINES GODLY WORSHIP, A CONTRAST TO WORSHIPPERS AT THYATIRA

According to Unger's "It is as natural to worship as it is to live. The feeling and expression of high adoration, reverence, trust, love, loyalty, and dependence upon a higher power, human or divine, is a necessity to man. Worship is as old as humanity."

No less authority than Jesus Christ speaking for the Old and New Testaments affirmed the question posed by a Jewish lawyer; to gain eternal life you must love God with all your heart, with all your soul, and with all your strength, and with all your mind (and your neighbor as yourself). Also God gave His only Son to the world so that whoever believes in Him, or worships Him, should not perish but have everlasting life. There is only one God; the God of Abraham, Isaac, and Jacob. Deuteronomy 6:4. The key words are love, love, love of God and Jesus and believe that Jesus is also God.

"Grace" is often described as God's unmerited favor for men and women. "Worship", it seems to me, is the merited favor offered freely by men and women to God in gratitude and love for His generosity and love for us.

The God of Israel and His Son require a new heart to love and worship. Both testaments are consistent; the New Testament speaks to being born of the Spirit where a believer who accepts Jesus' offer of eternal life to become a new person or a new creation who can now love and worship. The Old Testament required a "circumcised heart" to love and worship. Is there a difference; I don't think so.

God proved to His chosen people that He was God, the only God and through His commandments he warned that only He was to be worshipped based upon His miracles and He would give them a new heart to permit His chosen to love Him: "And the Lord your God will circumcise your heart and the heart of your descendants to love the Lord your God with all your heart and with all your soul, that you may live." Deuteronomy 30:6.

Men have always had a free-will to either love God and live, or reject God and perish. Everlasting life with Him was anticipated. David stated: "And I will dwell in the house of the Lord forever." Ps 23:6 and "The Lord redeems the soul of His servants. And none of those who trust in Him shall be condemned." Ps 34:22. Everlasting life; the miracle of miracles. Which is greater, everlasting life or the creation of the universe and everything in it that works predictably? Awesome, the whole thing!

Worship is based upon a personal relationship between the worshipper and God which is initiated by the Holy Spirit, washing the worshipper and in-dwelling the person with a new heart. We are specifically warned to not bow-down and serve idols (and false gods), which implies that we then must bow down and serve the Father, Son and Holy Spirit; or put another way, we must worship Them.

David, the "apple of God's eye", provides the Bible's example of how God must be worshipped, or the meaning of: "Worship only God".

Why was David the "apple of God's eye" considering that he was a polygamist, a poor father, an adulterer, and conspirator- murderer? His family was chaotic with too many wives and children, and he had no time or interest for family management, and preferential treatment for some of his children was endemic. His firstborn raped his half-sister and then he was subsequently murdered by David's favorite son, Absalom to avenge the rape of Tamar.

David, King of Israel, took advantage of his position and had sexual intercourse with the wife of a soldier in his army, Uriah the Hittite. Bathsheba conceived and David conspired to make it possible for Uriah to be the "father". The scheme failed so Uriah was ordered to the front lines where he was killed in battle as planned and expected, so that no one would know that he was not the father of the child carried by Bathsheba. God knew, however, and David was exposed a year later by Nathan the prophet.

In addition David was a courageous warrior, military leader, and planner. He was the Jewish model for their king and the Messiah that Jews through the ages longed for. Jesus had to be of the line of David but He disappointed when He came as a Lamb to take away the sins of the world. He will be King at His second coming.

What did David do to merit eternal life with God? He was a shepherd, warrior, leader, king, master-manager, poet, musician, adulterer, and murderer. He certainly worked very hard on behalf of his God. "Work" earns crowns but not eternal life. Moses brought us the law and the ten commandments, but David had a personal relationship with God and he also showed us how God wanted to be known and worshipped. This was David's greatest accomplishment and justification for eternal life with God. David never had a problem with idols like many of his compatriots. He recognized the name of God and worshipped only God: "O Lord GOD. For there is none like You, nor is there any God besides you—2 Samuel 7:22 " The angel said to John in the Book of Jesus: "Worship only God." David was faithful like no other; ever!

The Psalms and 2 Samuel give the account of David's fervor and total dependence upon God. Christians speak of a personal relationship with Jesus; what is meant by a personal relationship with God and what kind of a relationship does God want? David shows us by example in the Psalms. He spoke to God through prayer. His relationship was so close and intimate that he reverently chides God to "answer me when I call to you, O my righteous God—be merciful to me and hear my prayer— and I will lie down and sleep in peace, for you alone, make me dwell in safety ". Psalm 4.

David meditates upon God, loves God, worships God, and praises and praises his God for his very life and existence. He acknowledges God as his King and talks to God. He apparently meditates all night long because God is constantly on his mind; hence he makes requests of God in the morning and he expects an answer soon.

David proclaims in Psalm 23 that the Lord is his protector and leader and he has faith that he will provide for all his worldly needs and gives him rest no matter where he might be and his faith is continually restored. God's Spirit is always David's guide. Even in the worst conditions David is not fearful because he knows that he will not face the danger alone and David expects eternal life with God in His house.

David credits God in Psalm 24 to be the owner of the earth and it's inhabitants belong to only God. David knows that he can be with God by being washed to be "whiter than snow" through repentance and confession for his sin, and not bowing down and serving false gods or idols. David bows down and serves only God.

After his adultery with Bathsheba and the murder of Uriah, David acknowledges his sin and confesses to God only and appeals for forgiveness and restoration for the return of a joyful life, fellowship with God again, and service to God because he comes to God with a broken spirit. David bases his appeal on God's love for him even though he doesn't merit forgiveness as he has been sinful since birth. In the NT, also, a sinner-believer must have a broken contrite heart over his sin and he must acknowledge his need before God to find spiritual renewal or cleansing; it is called "confession." Psalm 51 stands as an example for us all, demonstrating prayers for the forgiveness of sin. God's Word needed Psalm 51 and David provided it in spades. Sadly, I've needed Psalm 51 far too often but believers through the ages have been comforted by the fact that since David's sins were forgiven theirs' can be too.

Concerning Psalm 51, David confesses only to God: "against thee only have I sinned", which is curious considering the harm to Bathsheba and her family. The Psalm suggests that the liaison with Bathsheba had been consensual so the affair was not odious to her. Also only God can forgive sin. David could express remorse to Bathsheba so that she could forgive his actions; but he didn't. Christians, in their haste without thinking, often forgive offenses or sin that in truth they cannot. For example, about five years ago a female prisoner was paraded on television just before her sentence was carried out for a murder she had been convicted of committing, before she had accepted Jesus. A leading Christian preacher declared that he could forgive her; he sounded merciful, but only God could forgive sin. She was executed.

David was created with an extremely rare combination of intelligence, courage, and creativity, coupled with passion. There may not have been anyone, ever, who had been so gifted—perhaps his son Solomon, or Superman. David did everything to excess; especially his lust for women. Even there he fought mightily, but he knew that it was not he, but the Holy Spirit who was convicting and guiding him out of trouble. In his great penitent Psalm 51, he begs God to not remove His Holy Spirit from him (David). Whereas other prophets come across as pious-holy men, David is real and experiences life; all of it, and yet he is the-apple-of-God's-eye. You can be sure that David was chastened for his behavior, but God in His love and mercy never removed His Holy Spirit from him. David worshipped only God which qualified him for eternal life with God. His sins were forgiven, not because of the blood of goats and burnt offerings, but because he approached God with a broken and contrite heart. Also, David was not a one time sinner who repented. Indeed, his life was a roller coaster of sin, repentance, and worship of his Lord and God with whom he had such a strong personal relationship every day, every night, every hour; and yet he still had time to sin. David didn't earn his way to eternal life by becoming more God-like; he just slowed down a wee-bit as he aged.

My testimony in the back of this book describes me as a Bapterian although I have also been exposed to the Roman Catholic Faith. Baptist and Presbyterian services have elements of the Psalms of David sprinkled throughout with music and spontaneous-fervent prayer to God. Obviously, God approved of David's enthusiasm for life as the Creator, but curbing his lust for life was a challenge, even for God.

David could never be portrayed as holy or pious, but he

was a great prophet nevertheless. He dwarfs contemporary giants like Reagan or Jefferson, Generals Patton or MacArthur, the Pope, or even Billy Graham or Johnny Cash. Some were political leaders, military warriors, religious leaders, or talented musicians; but none were wired in-total like David, a genetic miracle of creation. He represents one end of the humanity spectrum whereas Mary, the Mother of Jesus, has been shown to be a very-very Godly women with pious qualities and She represents the other end of the human spectrum. God loved them both; one was the apple-of-His-eye and the other was selected for the birth of His only Son when He was appointed to be sinless man upon the earth. Fortunately women were not created with the lust for life given men; David had it tough coping with his life.

Each Psalm of David has a similar message which shows elements of David's worship of God and character traits that God wants to be known by.

When addressing God in prayer use "O God" or "O Lord" as David did, but to say "O God" casually as we often hear friends, relatives, TV humorists, and movies show a lack of sensitivity and ignorance of Christian and Jewish values. Indeed, when spoken casually it is a blatant violation of the commandment "You shall not misuse the name of the Lord your God, for the Lord will not hold anyone guiltless who misuses His name. Dt. 5:11".

JESUS' CHURCH VI

Church at Laodicea; Jesus Minimized: in His Church

THE LUKEWARM CHURCH

"And to the church of the Laodiceans write:

> "These things says the Amen, the Faithful and True Witness,
> the Beginning of the creation of God: I know your works, that
> you are neither cold or hot. I could wish you were cold or hot.
> So then, because you are lukewarm, and neither cold or hot,
> I will vomit you out of My mouth.
>
> Because you say, I am rich, have become wealthy, and have
> need of nothing—and do not know that you are wretched,
> miserable, poor, blind, and naked—I council you to buy from
> Me gold refined in the fire, that you may be rich; and have
> white garments, that you may be clothed, that the shame of
> your nakedness may not be revealed; and anoint your eyes
> with eye salve, that you may see. As many as I love, I rebuke
> and chasten. Therefore be zealous and repent. Behold I stand
> at the door and knock. If anyone hears My voice and opens the
> door, I will come in to him and dine with him and He with
> Me. To him who overcomes I will grant to sit with Me on My
> throne, as I also sat down with my Father on His throne.
>
> He who has an ear, let him hear what the Spirit says to the
> churches"[51].

L AODICEA IS PORTRAYED BY JESUS as the lukewarm church, neither cold nor hot and He despises this church so much that He will vomit or spew it from His mouth. Unlike the church at Philadelphia that has an open door to Jesus and His Word that no one can shut, the door to the Laodicean church is shut to Him. In fact, He is outside what is supposed to be his own church knocking on their door requesting entry to the hearts of the Laodicean congregation. Whereas, Thyatira represents the Jesus plus other gods church, this church group represents the minus Jesus church. These people are as worldly as possible given their love of money, spiritual blindness, and prideful arrogance that they are self sufficient and don't need God.

Just a few short years previously Paul cited the Laodicean church with hope and encouragement[52] . He must to have been profoundly disappointed in the turn taken at Laodicea given that the head of all churches (Jesus) severely admonishes them.

The Laodicean church, prevalent at the end of the twentieth century, has the form or outward shape and appearance of Christianity and virtue referred to by Paul in Timothy and they are without any merit whatever:

"But know this, that in the last days perilous times will come: For men will be lovers of themselves, lovers of money, boasters, proud, blasphemers, disobedient to parents, unthankful, unholy, unloving, unforgiving, slanderers, without self-control, brutal, despisers of good, traitors, headstrong, haughty, lovers of pleasure, rather than lovers of God, having a form of godliness but denying its power "[53].

This church is no different than the world. Born of the Spirit? Perhaps Satan.

Jesus councils the other church types to listen to Him. In addition He also admonishes this church to open their eyes as well. But there are those in Laodicea that may overcome even their situation in this church and be clothed in white with those from the church of Philadelphia.

JESUS' CHURCH VII

CHURCH AT EPHESUS: INDIFFERENCE AND MALAISE TO JESUS IN HIS CHURCH

THE LOVELESS CHURCH

To the angel at the Church at Ephesus write:

"These things says He who holds the seven stars in His right hand, who walks in the midst of the seven golden lamp stands: I know your works, your labor, your patience, and you cannot bear those who are evil. And you have tested those who say they are apostles and are not, and have found them liars; and you have persevered and have patience, and have labored for My name's sake and have not become weary. Nevertheless I have this against you, that you have left your first love. Remember therefore from where you have fallen; repent and do the first works, or else I will come to you quickly and remove your lamp stand from its place—unless you repent. But this you have, that you hate the deeds of the Nicolaitans, which I also hate.
He who has an ear, let him hear what the Spirit says to the churches. To him who overcomes I will give to eat from the tree of life, which is in the midst of the Paradise of God." [54].

SEVEN STARS REPRESENT MESSENGERS TO the seven churches and the seven lamp stands represent the seven churches Jesus presents for the ages. "Seven" is significant because it represents completeness so that there are only seven possible church types that Jesus presents: the faithful church, the persecuted church, the dead church without the Holy Spirit, the compromising church imbedded with phony leadership, the corrupt church who have included idolatry or more than Jesus, the lukewarm materialistic church that doesn't need much of Jesus, and finally, the loveless church that suffers from disinterest concerning the Savior. When Jesus portrays His church in scripture, He can only be referring to the "faithful' and "persecuted" churches, and faithful remnants of the deviate churches.

In its favor, Ephesus did not tolerate sin within the church and hated the deeds of the Nicolaitans, as did the Lord Jesus. Whatever doctrine the Nicolaitans were actively advocating, it was unnecessary and in addition to "Jesus and His Word"; He will permit no more and no less. It is interesting that the Lord hates their deeds, but not the Nicolaitans personally. He is always consistent to hate the sin but not the sinner; even Nicolaitans.

The church at Ephesus, or a church of this type, may not be permitted to exist at all if it abandons its first love, Jesus Christ. That is, the "lamp stand" will be removed. According to the publication: Israel My Glory , the Ephesian church closed in the fifth century. This church had many advantages having been personally ministered to by Paul for a period of three years, and in its formative years it was the mother church for other churches in Asia Minor. Nevertheless, it fell away from its first love, Jesus Christ, and its lamp stand was removed.

The church at Ephesus was ministered to by Paul as he spread the "word" as commanded by the Lord Jesus just before He ascended into heaven: "Go into all the world and preach the gospel to all creation. Whoever believes and is baptized will be saved, but whoever does not believe will be condemned." Mark 16:15,16. At first, the church at Ephesus spread the gospel and established new churches. Apparently, evangelism is the charter for every church. It is not an accident that John discusses this church first, of the seven churches.

The purposes of gathering together believers to form a church (a group of believers), any church:

- honoring God through prayer, praise, and worship, emphasizing the name of Jesus, learning about Him and His message,
- encouraging and providing family love for one another of the church, or love of the brethren,
- evangelizing neighborhoods, branching outward to adjacent regions even to the ends of the earth,
- equipping worshippers to evangelize others,
- providing a Christian illustration of brotherly and neighborly love to the world.

Without evangelism, the church at Ephesus, or anywhere else will eventually fail. Evangelism is necessary for any healthful church who values it's charter with the One who walks amid the golden lamp stands. Basically, Jesus is pleased with the church except it has lost sight of it's mission --- it has lost it's way and unless it repents and finds it's way, it will be allowed to deteriorate and desist. I re-arranged the order of presentation to emphasize a truly acceptable church, the church at Philadelphia. The biblical chronology, listing the Church at Ephesus first may have been of more importance to Jesus than supposed, as evangelism is very high amongst Jesus' priorities. It is speculated that He will remove their lamp stand if they do not return to their charter—and the charter of every church.

The lamp stand of any or every church, as small as a Bible study group for that matter, which fails to evangelize, or spread the Word or Good News will eventually lose their charter, or lamp stand representing a church. It is impossible to see how a healthy Christ could live in a church which fails to teach Him to unbelievers—of course Jesus will no longer walk amongst their lamp stands.

If indeed these churches represent various periods of the church of Jesus Christ as some believe, then it may be of interest that the first church at Ephesus after awhile, became like the last church at Laodicea; Christ is minimized or marginalized. Ephesus is often referred to as the "loveless church"; like Laodicea it too, it might be characterized as without Jesus and hence love, as God is love[55].

JESUS' CHURCH VIII

SUMMARY

THE RELATIVELY FEW BELIEVERS OF the Churches at Philadelphia and Smyrna and the faithful remnant of the churches at Sardis, Pergamos, Thyatira, Laodicea, and Ephesus that kept His word and did not deny His name, will be raised having died in Christ and if alive, kept from the "great tribulation" at the trump of God. The majority of the folks of these representative churches are today awaiting judgment on the Day of the Lord, or after the "great tribulation". Jesus knew that the majority of His so-called followers would be without the Holy Spirit and spiritually dead, contaminated, corrupt, lukewarm, or indifferent to Him and the Scriptures.

Given the record of the "churches", one must conclude that many pastors and denominations through the ages have not really been on the Lord's side. Who's side then have they been on! Philadelphia believers are few in number and all Christians can expect to be persecuted to some degree. That is, in this day, the churches of Philadelphia and Smyrna are indeed one church and are the only bodies of believers that are on the Lord's side. Pastors and elders that are dead in Christ, contaminated with politics, corrupted by their idol worship rather than Jesus, and unbelief are solemnly charged by God to be teachers and shepherds of their flocks. What defense will Biblically trained people offer on the Day of the Lord.

The term "born-again" Christian is really an oxymoron; however, it seems obvious that church leadership at Sardis, Pergamos, Thyatira, Laodicea, and Ephesus are neither "born-again" and hence, not even Christian although they minister to Jesus' "Christian" churches. Surely they met the qualifications specified for leadership, but they didn't comprehend the meaning of the spiritual birth (regeneration) or the Sermon on the Mount, which are basic to Christianity. There would be no degenerate congregations if the shepherds and their flocks were "born-again" and hence, Christians.

Contemporarily there are congregations that combine all of the attributes of Sardis, Pergamos, Laodicea, and Ephesus at once being dead to the Holy Spirit, contaminated with politics and the world, and lukewarm to the Savior of the world. Thyatirian congregations are still corrupting worship and raise up other gods to rival the Son of Man. The dragnet parable describes the situation at the end of this age when God will separate the just from the unjust: a picture describing the contrast between the church at Philadelphia and Sardis, Pergamos, Thyatira, Laodicea, Ephesus, and the world [56].

God, in His disgust, over the issues of denial of His power, the creation, and worship of false gods and idols gave men up to "vile passions" and "shameful lusts" which are described in Paul's letter to the Romans. God let us wallow in our sin. The solution is obvious: worship God and live, but worship false gods and idols and perish.

The message for the churches is to stand firm in the faith, remember His name (Jesus), and uphold His Word in the scriptures! Nothing more and nothing less; do not add or subtract from the Word of God. A remnant of believers at Sardis, Pergamos, Thyatira, Laodicea, and Ephesus will be saved, but why should the children of God settle as remnants when they can be "pillars" in heaven from the Church at Philadelphia.

Just as important as to what "Philadelphia" has, are some of the adverse traits that it does not have. It is not spiritually dead with corrupt leadership, contaminated with the worldly pursuits, and lukewarm to Jesus and the scriptures. "Philadelphia" is focused upon the Son of God and our Father. A church, however, must be ever vigilant lest "yeast" enter and influence church leadership.

Keep in mind the words of John 3:16, if anyone thinks that God is selective: "For God so loved the world, that He gave His only begotten Son, that **whosoever** believeth in Him should not perish but have everlasting life." That is, everyone is in the Book of Life until one either agrees that the Holy Spirit seal it forever, or decides that he would rather have his name blotted out by rejecting God and His Son. "His yoke is easy and His burden is light" and His message is simple and if it were not so He would have told us.

The Book of Jesus speaks to events that will occur at the end of the age. Therefore, the picture that Jesus gives regarding His churches most likely applies to this time mostly and not just some church problems of the first century. Pastors have "neglected speaking to the "churches" and hence have contributed to churches today not conforming to God's perfect will"[1]. It is noteworthy that Jesus himself had the last word in the Scriptures; not Peter, nor Luke, nor James, nor John, or even Paul the theologian. All of the Bible is God's inspired word, but Jesus finished the account of God.

Subsequently John is raptured to heaven where he writes what he sees surrounding the throne of God.

JESUS' CHURCH

EPILOGUE

WINTERS, WE WORSHIP AT SURFSIDE (PCA) in Surfside Beach, S.C., just south of Myrtle Beach, S.C., in Horry County, which is definitely better than it sounds. It has a powerful witness for Christ on the Grand Strand with a motto: "Where Christ is pre-eminent". We have two services; one contemporary and one traditional. The pastor is a former football coach who, in everything, "leaves everything on the field". In addition to the two services on Sunday, he does two Bible studies on Tuesday, every week for the entire year. His retired men's study have about 40 regular attendees: a former bounty hunter, union leader, coal miner, prison guard, several engineers, bartender, car salesman, naval submariner, missionaries on leave, a retired 98 years young African missionary, accountant, farmer, prison missionary, security guard, FBI agent, physicist, another former football coach etc. These guys are born-again sinners with purpose. He lives, and everyone has a testimony.

Wednesday evening is Bible study and party (fellowship) night at the Snyder's. Dave's chart was stamped twice after his heart stopped fifteen years ago after his doctor only gave him six months. An "angel" told him to not get on the "carpet". Dave and Raeanne lost their home to a fire four years ago. Insurance and the church provided and they now conduct our

Wednesday studies in their triple-wide which was designed by Raeanne. They have been twice married, to each other. Our teacher is John Givens, a retired Baptist preacher from Presbyterian Princeton; how unusual is that. There are about twenty attendees at the weekly study of God's Word at the Snyder's.

Basically, our Huntington Beach ministry provide Sunday services each summer for campers at Huntington Beach State Park, which is nearby. This ministry has been fathered by one Jim Dove, the Myrtle Beach Volunteer Man of the Year for 2005 for his community contributions. Preaching by John Givens and others is inspirational, loving, and reasoned. Jim, a retired engineer, lost his dear wife Mary Belle Dove three years ago. She ran the Surfside "Helping Hand" ministry, where she had also been nominated for "Man of the Year". Jim will always be my "elder". Lib Huckabee and Jim are now partners and friends.

Jim Doe (not our Jim Dove), a young father, needs a kidney. Ten worshippers have offered Jim theirs'; only one has been selected for this on-going saga of this loving church. We are not members, but we have been involved for about 11 years; I write this as a northern astonished observer of a group of people who truly love the Lord Jesus, the brethren and their neighbors. Several years ago a severe hurricane devastated the tiny central American country of Belize; at the close of the Sunday service thirty-five hundred dollars were on their way to our missionary there. Surfside PCA people know where they are going.

Worshipers, and the leadership, have all experienced a second birth—a distinguishing feature. You know them by their fruits. They recognize that they are sinners, especially before they accepted Jesus as Lord and Savior and they hunger and thirst for the Word of God. Evangelical: yes! The congregation is mostly Presbyterian and Baptist and therefore somewhat Bapterian, although most would like to be identified just as "Christian".

No finer tribute could be given to a "Christian Church" than to be called out as representative of the Church of Philadelphia. The evidence is in and Surfside Presbyterian Church (PCA) is qualified as a "Church of Philadelphia". Their sign on highway 17 bypass could be pride-fully changed to read:

SURFSIDE PRESBYTERIAN CHURCH
(PCA AND JESUS' CHURCH)

Many years ago, while I was on assignment to Washington D.C. we attended a Brethren Church in Temple Hills, Md.. Grace Brethren Church of Temple Hills also was representative of the Church of Philadelphia as recorded by John in the Book of Jesus. The denomination is unimportant so long as there is not more or less doctrine than Jesus crucified for our transgressions.

"Jesus' Church and the Book of Life" is my attempt to: "walk on water, you must get out of the boat". I am in theological territory that most professionals treat lightly or not at all. Hence, this book may be useful to possibly answer some questions concerning our God, even after two thousand years. The printing press made the Bible available to all for the last five hundred years; enough time to conclude that we only need to "worship God".

My testimony is modest, and or typical, and it has been included in this epilogue. Perhaps you have had similar experiences in your "walk".

Testimony of Albert J. Kausch, January, 2007

I CAME TO BELIEVE THAT JESUS Christ is the Son of God and that He was sacrificed on the cross for my transgressions, or sins, and He was buried and rose from the grave and today he is on the right hand of our Father where He judges those who do not accept Him and He acts as our advocate with our Father for those who do believe Him or worship Him as our God. I acknowledge that I am a sinner and deserve only condemnation and I am truly sorry for the sin and grief I have caused the Holy Spirit, my neighbors, and my wife and children. All sin has consequences.

I was given a choice to live and follow a loving God, or die and follow a deceitful adversary; Satan, by name. I joined with Jesus and the Father at a David Wilkerson crusade service in Schenectady, N.Y. on October 2, 1969 where I was born of the Spirit, forever sealing my name in the Lamb's Book of Life. This decision and my marriage to my bride are the most significant events in my life. Nothing happens by chance, my romance and both marriages are related as even then God was looking out for me. I came to Jesus, or Jesus came to me when I was 40 years old, but we are told that: "the last will be first and the first will be last". It's never too late to make the choice and acknowledge before men that Jesus is Lord. Remember the thief on the cross; that day he was with Jesus in paradise after simply acknowledging Jesus as Lord. Give up pride and gain eternal life; an unbelievable bargain which is so simple but so hard.

I was born and raised in Rochester, N.Y.. At least three times in my life, angels of God protected me to permit me to come to this point in my life: "to save a wretch like me! I once was lost but now am found, Was blind but now I see.—Tis grace hath brought me safe thus far, and grace will lead me home." Simply put, God wasn't finished with me when at the age of five, I started to cross Norton Street in Rochester. My dear mother told me that I woke up three days later after having been hit by a car that I never saw nor remembered. I had a concussion but there was no fracture.

The year I graduated from high school, after a night of carousing, I caught a foul ball on the thumb of my throwing hand causing a compound fracture of the thumb and a nerve problem in the thumb that prevented me from taking a "cut" without pain. It's hard to hit with wooden bats that sting, with sore hands. I didn't know it at the time but that was the end of a baseball career that never really was a career. I loved and understood baseball better than anything else I knew. But God had other plans.

Years later, I was in the woods in the Adirondacks working on a heavy log stairway leading to the front porch. I was standing on the stairway when it slipped from beneath me and I was airborne to come down on the fallen steps. The time of my fall must have been only micro-seconds, but somehow I turned slightly in the air. Two ribs were broken in the middle of my back, one inch from my spine, as I came down on the lethal edge of the steps that were now on the ground. The ribs punctured my lungs, but my heart and spine were ok. Helen comforted me and summoned an ambulance crew into the woods. Breathing was tough with a collapsed lung and it took a week to clean the hemlock needles from my bed that were stuck to my "woods clothes". Glens Falls Hospital does a good job with the basics but there are no frills. I was afraid to move as I had no idea where the ends of those jagged ribs were, but nevertheless a nurse made me walk the next day. More angels looking out for Albert J..

During high school I had a part-time job tending bar about 40 hours a week, and another one at an A&P meat market on Saturday. I worked hard, played hard, and studied little. I was a candidate for reform school and or prison. After high school, I tried my hand at playing professional baseball where I found out the awful truth that I was good field but no hit, which is actually very common. Baseball is all about "hitting" and "throwing" and as a position player I was expected to hit. I became a pitcher, a very good pitcher, at the age of 21 which was too late in those days. Actually I was in the popcorn machine of life which took many twists and turns ---- philosophically I can now look back and see where God opened and closed career opportunities and relationships. Somehow I was accepted, or rescued, by a very good engineering school. I made the most of this final opportunity; no one was ever more determined to escape the pop-corn machine.

I graduated from NY State Maritime College as an engineer, also with a marine license for steam or Diesel for any tonnage for any ocean. Henceforth I went to work with GE for a couple of months, and then went into the Navy serving on minesweepers at sea in the Pacific for two years. Eager for graduate school I went back to GE, first to the Flight Propulsion Laboratory in Evandale, Ohio, and then to Knolls Atomic Power Laboratory in Schenectady, NY for the next 35 years where I helped design nuclear powered submarines. I also evaluated Soviet submarine concepts during the "cold war". Along the way, I got my master's degree from Rensselaer Polytechnic Institute in Troy, NY.

During those years I built a summer home in the woods on Friend's Lake, which is Atateka to the Mohawk-Iroquois in the Adirondack Mountains. It was there that the aforementioned accident with my porch steps occurred. Water-color painting became a serious hobby.

I came to realize that work and achievement were like chasing windmills; there was no end to it and no lasting satisfaction or anchor. I was a successful achiever with a very good technical reputation. I was the manager of a Navy skunk-works dedicated to Advanced Development of nuclear power for submarines. One night we were bringing a new reactor on-line and while reading some data, I apparently took the name of our Lord in vain. A nearby engineer told me that I had offended him. I never imagined or dreamt that I offended anyone. A few weeks later I was told during a basketball game in a GE league that I "had a dirty mouth". There was no argument but still I was shocked, but apparently it was true ---- I was ok to my friends but obnoxious to "Christians". Not long thereafter I became a believer. There were changes and I studied the Bible and served in a fundamentalist evangelical church where I had some success and some spiritual failures; my trajectory was sometimes up and sometimes down. The Holy Spirit nagged me for many-many years as I continued to grieve him. You might say that I was a "lukewarm" Christian. We know that Jesus has little regard for the lukewarm church represented by the church at Laodicea, but I was always aware that I had said "I do" to the Lord Jesus, and hence married forever. I, nor anyone, can break the bond. Satan pursues Christians to ruin their witness, but I didn't belong to him.

With that background, I would like to share my recent testimony with you. I had my right hip replaced in 1992. Eight years later it was determined that plastic wear particles from the rubbing surface of the socket had attacked the bone in my pelvis causing a hole about three inches in diameter. Pain was considerable, but more important only a rim of solid bone supported the artificial socket; even slight weight on the joint could cause it to fracture.

The pelvis is the large elemental bone that unites the body's support system; that is, the legs and body come together at the pelvis. The circulatory system needs the heart and the structural system of bones needs a healthy pelvis. During the summer of 2000, cat-scans and x-rays revealed that my pelvis on the right side was rotten—decayed—deteriorated.

The Lord arranged my surgery for the Lahey Clinic, in a suburb of Boston, with a doctor who thought there to be some chance to get the old hardware out without breaking the rim of solid bone, put in a new graft of bone that lives, replace and hold the socket with something he called a cage, and screws and then rehabilitate me for about three months while the bone graft got life and became a structural hip again. The hardware needed to stay together until the graft material hardened, like the rest of the pelvis.

The surgery took six-hours as the doctors literally rebuilt my pelvis and put in hardware designed and fitted as he went along. Because of the length of the surgery, gases contained in the anesthesia tended to appear as a lot of poison in my system. Also, narcotics taken to relieve pain added to the poisons and further complications. I became very ill; my stomach and intestines stopped functioning. Also my intestines were attacked by a nasty bacteria that caused great bloating and pain. For three long weeks my bones ached, worms lived in my bowels, and my tongue clung to the roof of my dry-parched mouth; the pain never left. I still had to be mindful of hip and pelvis precautions so that the new construction would not dislocate. I was somewhere in the middle between life and death. My brain was functioning and it told me that I was very messed up. One-hundred Canadians died in 2005 in one hospital in Quebec from the bacteria that called me home.

Brothers and sisters of three churches were in earnest prayer for my surgery and healing; East Glenville Community Church of Glenville, N.Y., The PCA of Surfside Beach, South Carolina, and Loudonville Community Church, near Albany, N.Y.

People question the reality of God and even Christians would like to know his whereabouts; or where is God and when does He show up. I can say with confidence that in my situation I knew that God was present because I had no anxiety or fear. Generally I am not immune to these emotions, but for my stay at Lahey in those painful dark hours I knew that God was present because there was an absence of fear or anxiety in a situation that would normally have called for fear.

Also, when you endure suffering you suffer alone, but again you know the presence of God because He will be your only comfort. You're either going to get better or worse and I couldn't do anything about it except to rely upon His Word that: "He would never leave me nor forsake me".

In my suffering, I cried a lot out of gratefulness to God for sending His attending angels, my nurses and doctors, my family who was with me through it all, and my dear friends who ministered to me through prayer. Some of those friends are so close to me that they are family indeed.

One night a tall, slim, Chinese doctor, dressed in green operating room garb appeared unsolicited and she re-positioned my stomach tube so that the end in my stomach was in the right place to properly drain my stomach She said: "there you will feel better now". She came to me twice; I never saw her again. Yes, I believe in Chinese angels.

> *"Yea thou I walk through the valley of the shadow of death,*
> **I will fear no evil;**
> **For You are with me;**
> *Your rod and your staff they comfort me."*

Indeed the Psalm is true. I know that God was present because there was an absence of fear and He gave resolve and comfort. He was my only comfort, especially in the middle of the night when pain and suffering are worst. I welcomed the tubes and shunts and very hard x-ray tables; bring it on, we can take it; Jesus and me.

Six weeks after the surgery, my doctor was "surprised" to see on x-ray the healing that had taken place in the bone graft and that all eight of four-inch screws were in place. After twelve weeks he thought the healing to be unexplainable. My healing was indeed a miracle fashioned by God answering the fervent prayers of His people in my behalf. Why has God been so good to me; or why me. Typically, "victims" lament over misfortune or "why me". I am grateful that God created my body and mind and that they have lasted as long as they have. It took a year for the bone graft to harden.

It has been five years since the surgery and all eight screws are still tight. We tend to not remember pain the way it happened so I wrote it down so that I would not forget the experience. In the hospital bed in Boston, the den of modern liberalism, I was forced to listen to twenty-four hour CNN news covering the election of Geo. W. Bush and the shenanigans of the Florida Supreme Court. So in addition to my physical problems there were TV talking head induced mental problems as well.

Each of us will be tried in some manner; life is that way, it will happen and our God will be there for us. It will happen to me again, perhaps several times. I can't imagine how unbelievers cope with pain and tragedy.

It is important to me that I give thanks to God for delivering me in my time of trouble and praise the Lord and acknowledge his Holy name:

He says in Psalm 116:12-14:

"What shall I render to the Lord
For all His benefits toward me?
I will take up the cup of salvation,
And will call upon the name of the Lord.
I will pay my vows to the Lord
Now in the presence of all His people".

For my testimony to be complete, I must discus our children's problems which of course became our problems. Daughter Susan when she was ten, was struck by an automobile while crossing route 50 on her bike breaking her leg and ruining her bike. She recovered completely and many years later graduated from the University of Buffalo as a Physical Therapist. From there she entered medical school, but she became afflicted with Multiple Sclerosis in her first year. The disease affected her eyesight; several times losing sight, but each time it has come back but always with some reduction. Sue has reduced energy to a level which is now similar to most people. Her trust is in the Lord and God has more plans for Sue and she lives life to the fullest walking with the Lord. Susan is a practicing psychiatrist working with and for the indigent in Albany, NY. Her family have taken two vacation-short term mission trips to Belize. Susan and John will one day retire to the mission field and or Camp-of- the-Woods, a Christian vacation camp, in Speculator, NY.

It was not God's plan that son Albert Paul would be blinded at the age of fifteen when he was struck with a thrown rock while swimming at our summer home at Friend's Lake. We brought him to a hospital 70 miles away and found an eye specialist on the fourth-of- July, a miracle by itself, that treated and advised Albert to not move his head for three weeks. Everyone prayed and the Lord kept Albert and he did not move for three weeks. Doctor Green, a dedicated wonderful Jewish doctor removed the bandages and Albert could see. Today Albert Paul is a PhD world class scientist that has been awarded twenty-three patents in plant genetics and he is a tenured professor at the University of Rhode Island. We hold to the promise that "none will be lost, no not one" as Albert belonged to God in those days so long ago. Check out Albert Paul's educational tutorial on DNA for everyone in WWWLIFEEDU.ORG and love our Jewish brethren and especially Jewish doctors who work on July 4th .

Joseph, at the age of six, stepped behind a stout tree as a huge sixty foot maple I was dropping came crashing beside him. How or why did Joseph just step in an instant behind that tree. He was a little kid watching Dad with his chain saw in the woods; I didn't know that he was there and I had my tree on my mind.

Then, a couple of years latter I had my lawn mower on blocks changing oil and cleaning clippings off the underside of the machine. For some reason, the blade nut was loosened. The machine was tipped back so that the front was off the ground and I started it. Joseph was watching. The blade was thrown from the machine and it shot between little Joe's legs right through the garage wall. It left a clean one-half by three inch hole and we picked up the missile in the back yard. The spinning blade never touched the lad. The Lord protected me and Joseph; I was sparred a lifetime of grief and Joseph never knew that the blade shot between his legs. It would have surely been as deadly as a three inch missile. Praise the Lord for His gracious protection. The Lord had other plans for Joseph.

After retirement in 1993 we sold the summer home and acquired a winter residence condo at a resort in wonderful South Carolina where I now write essays supporting God and conservative values via the newspaper, go to ball games, and paint Christmas cards with a Jesus' message. I send out about a hundred cards and I give them away literally at cost; it has become a ministry because cards, appropriate for the season, are no longer available.

Baseball is my passion but Jesus is my Savior and the Holy Spirit is my guide in the maze of life who too often must chasten my walk, even now:

Bartender
Ballplayer
Meat cutter
Naval Officer
Engineer
Builder
Essayist
Artist
Father
Husband
Christian

Thank you for listening and thank you Lord.

Albert J. Kausch

JESUS' CHURCH

References:

1. The Bible Knowledge Commentary of the Old and New Testament by John F. Walvoord and Roy B. Zuck; 1989

2. Slouching Toward Gomorrah by Robert Bork.

3. Revelation 3: 7-12.

4. John 6:39

5. Revelation 3:20

6. Matt 16:18

7. Eph 5:25.

8. Refer to Matt 5:3-12 which is called the Beatitudes

9. I Timothy 3.

10. Titus 1:5-9

11. Matt 13: 45-46.

12. Revelation 2:8-11.

13. John 15:18

14. 2 Timothy 3:12.

15. John 15:23.

16. Matt 12:30

17. Genesis 3:15

18. Revelation 3:1-6.

19. 2Cor 4:3

20. Exodus 32: 31-33

21. Ungers Bible Dictionary

22. John 6:39

23. Psalm 139:15-17.

24. Ezekiel 20:27-28.

25. Luke: 10: 25-28

26. Deut. 6:5 and Lev. 19:18.

27. Ex. 20:3-4.

28. Ps 24:3-4.

29. Ps 51

30. Deuteronomy 30:15-18

31. The MacArthur Study Bible: New King James version.

32. Matt 17

33. John 14:6

34. John 3:16.

35. Ephesians 1:13-14

36. John 18:9

37. Matt 25: 31-46

38. Revelation 2:12-17

39. Acts 4:12

40. Philippians 2:9-11.

41. Revelation 2: 18-29

42. 1Kings 16:30.

43. 1Kings 21:25-26.

44. 2Kings 9: 22.

45. Acts: 10:25-26.

46. Acts: 14: 15-18

47. Revelation 19:10.

48. Jude 24-25.

49. Revelation 3:8

50. Revelation 22:18-19.

51. Revelation 3:14-22.

52. Colossians 4:13 and Colossians 4:16

53. 2 Timothy 3: 1-5.

54. Revelation 2:1-7.

55. 1 John 4:16.

56. Matt 13:47-50.

57. 1Kings 19:18

58. Romans 10: 11-13.

ISBN 142510324-3